D0849918

LIVING THE TRUTH
IN A WORLD OF ILLUSIONS

OTHER BOOKS BY WILLIAM SLOANE COFFIN

The Courage to Love
Once to Every Man

# Living the Truth in a World of Illusions

William Sloane Coffin

*1817*

Harper & Row, Publishers, San Francisco

Cambridge, Hagerstown, New York, Philadelphia
London, Mexico City, São Paulo, Singapore, Sydney

*To Randy*

Scripture quotations, unless otherwise noted, are from the *Revised Standard Version* of the Bible, Old Testament Section, Copyright 1952; New Testament Section, First Edition, Copyright 1946; Second Edition © 1971 by Division of Christian Education of the National Council of Churches of Christ in the United States of America.

Acknowledgment is made for the following: an excerpt from "Do not go gentle into that good night" by Dylan Thomas from *Poems of Dylan Thomas*. Copyright 1952 by Dylan Thomas. Reprinted by permission of New Directions Publishing Corporation; excerpts from *Four Quartets* by T. S. Eliot, copyright 1943 by T. S. Eliot, renewed 1971 by Esme Valerie Eliot. Reprinted by permission of Harcourt Brace Jovanovich, Inc.

FIRST EDITION

---

Library of Congress Cataloging in Publication Data

Coffin, William Sloane.
    Living the truth in a world of illusions.

    Includes index.
    1. Church and the world—Sermons. 2. Sermons, American. 3. Reformed Church—Sermons. I. Title.
BR115.W6C59  1985      252'.051      84-48766
ISBN 0-06-061512-5

---

85  86  87  88  89  HC  10  9  8  7  6  5  4  3  2  1

# Contents

# Preface

I believe the Christian faith seeks less to define what is right and wrong than to establish what is good and evil. It seeks as much to fan the flame of creativity as to quench the fires of sin. I believe Christ became like us that we might become more like him—full of love and courage, those virtues that make all other virtues possible.

I also believe strongly that in the United States, and in the world today, systems need to be converted as well as individuals; our sins are social as much as they are personal. Therefore, I believe God wants the churches more than ever to plead the cause of the poor and needy, and to seek peace by reversing an arms race that presently has the entire planet on a count-down to destruction. In a world full of illusions, God wants Christians to live the truth as honestly as they can, perhaps as Karl Barth suggested, Bible in one hand, a newspaper in the other.

In any case, that's what many, if not all, of these sermons are about. I have arranged them loosely around the celebrations and themes of the faith, from Advent to Reformation Sunday, traditionally the last Sunday in October.

To me, preaching is raising to a conscious level the knowledge inherent in everyone's experience. As in a good "whodunit," so in a good sermon, surprise is the discovery of inevitability. If readers of this book occasionally exclaim, "Of course," the writer will be delighted. I should add that while most preachers are incurable magpies, I am a shameless one, especially when it comes to my friends and my favorite biblical commentator William Barclay.

# 1. What Kind of Obedience to What Kind of God?

Readings: Isaiah 9:6–7
Luke 2:8–12

There are two versions of Christianity so out of step with Christmas that one of these years Christmas will put them out of business. The first is joyless Christianity. Nietzsche said, "Christians should look more redeemed." He was right: too many of us have just enough religion to make ourselves miserable! Joyless Christians tend to deify not God, but their own virtue. They tend to be Victorian rather than Elizabethan. Pretending to be upright, they really are uptight. And that's what makes joyless Christianity no laughing matter, for those who are themselves repressed become themselves repressive.

A second kind of Christianity that comes out all wrong at Christmas is "authoritarian" as opposed to "humanitarian" Christianity. To followers of authoritarian Christianity, God's power is more important than God's love, and self-denial more important than self-realization. In authoritarian Christianity the cardinal sin is not a refusal to love, but a failure to obey norms of thought and behavior fixed by someone else in some other time. And the followers of authoritarian Christianity tend to be reactionary. The goal of life, as they see it, is less to change the world than to reproduce it, generally according to an earlier and presumably simpler model.

In everybody's version of Christianity obedience plays a central role. The poet Schiller wrote:

> Courage can be shown by any fool
> Obedience is the Christian's jewel.

But what kind of obedience are we talking about, and to what kind of God? Surely there is a difference between discerning obedience and blind obedience. Discerning obedience I can understand as a legitimate religious concept, and in a world full of the mysteries of pain and death, I can see trusting where I cannot understand. But blind obedience I can't understand at all. Abraham's willingness, for example, to sacrifice his son Isaac I find totally incomprehensible, not to say reprehensible. How could Abraham have conceived God's love to be something less than human love as we know it at its best? Actually, one interpretation in Jewish expository literature (Midrash) says that God was so disgusted with Abraham's blind obedience to what he misconceived to be God's will that God hastily dispatched a ram to save Isaac's life, and swore never to speak to Abraham again, which in the Bible God never does.

In a book as provocative as its title, *Beyond Mere Obedience*, German theologian Dorothee Soelle explains that she has trouble with the notion of obedience on three counts: She is a German, she is a Christian, and she is a woman. (Let no American feel superior, for Lord knows we too have fought, killed, and died in blind obedience to wrong causes.) After saying that she has simply seen too many people give over their reason and conscience to someone else, Soelle asks a telling question: Can you require unquestioning obedience to God, and then criticize the same stance when it comes to other people, institutions, and one's own nation? To make her point, she quotes the following confession.

I was brought up by my parents to give due respect and honor to all adults, particularly older persons, no matter which social classes they belonged to. Wherever the need arose, I was told it was my primary duty to be of assistance. In particular I was always directed to carry out the wishes and directives of my parents, the teacher, pastor, in fact of all adults including household servants, without hesitation, and allow nothing to deter me. What such persons said was always right. Those rules of conduct have become part of my very flesh and blood.

With this strict "Christian" upbringing the author of the above lines, Rudolph Hoess, went on to become, for three years, the director of the infamous Auschwitz concentration camp.

What kind of obedience to what kind of God? These are the questions answered at Christmas. At Christmas the Word of the Lord hits the world with the force of a hint—a babe in a manger. Why would the all-powerful God in whom Christians believe ever want to come to earth in this fashion?

The answer is suggested by the fable of the king who fell in love with a maid. When asked, "How shall I declare my love?" his counselors answered, "Your majesty has only to appear in all the glory of your royal raiments before the maid's humble abode and she will instantly fall at your feet and be yours."

But it was precisely that thought that so troubled the king. He wanted her glorification, not his. In return for his love he wanted hers, freely given. The one thing he did not want was her submission to his power. What a dilemma, when not to declare his love spelled the end of love, and to declare it spelled the end of his beloved! Finally, the king realized love's truth, that freedom for the beloved demanded equality with the beloved. So late one night, after all the counselors and courtiers of the palace had retired, he stole out a side door and appeared before the maid's cottage dressed as a servant.

Clearly, the fable is a Christmas story. But before we get carried away by this imaginative, loving king, let us realize that the story, so satisfactory to its hero, and to its author, Søren Kierkegaard, might well have been anything but satisfactory to its heroine. Had I been the maid, I would have wanted to know more about this stranger who appeared at my door, more about his future and mine. Was I to be stuck forever in the servant's quarters? Come to think of it, I don't mind a little submission. I don't mind marrying a king!

Likewise, before we gush about the King of Kings born among beasts in a stall, let us recognize that we too would have preferred God to remain God, rather than become the frailest among us. We want God to be strong so that we can be weak. But God wants to be weak so that we can be strong.

I understand Isaiah's frustration when he cried out, "O that thou wouldst rend the heavens and come down . . . that the nations might tremble at thy presence" (Isa. 64:1, 2). But no such thing. At Christmas, God puts himself at our mercy: Why, we could crack that baby's head like an eggshell! Imagine! God is not safe from us, we have to protect God. And I think I see why: God had to come to earth as a child so that you and I might finally grow up. That's the Christmas message that one of these years is going to put authoritarian Christianity out of business.

The trouble with the usual notion of Christian obedience is that it sees obedience in relation to God's power, rather than to God's love. It overlooks the truth grasped finally by the loving king, that freedom for the beloved requires equality with the beloved. The trouble with the usual notion of Christian obedience is that it represents a childhood model of living. Fearing confusion, a child naturally wants supervision and direction. A child wants a superior power to provide order, to direct its destiny—and so do childish adults. But let's face that desire and call it what it is—a temptation to disobedience. For we are called to obey not God's power, but God's love. God wants not submission to his power, but in return for his love, our own.

God comes to earth as a child so that you and I and every other adult might finally grow up. Many of us will, in this Advent season, see once again Menotti's "Amahl and the Night Visitors." Amahl, the crippled boy, is miraculously cured when he himself gives to the infant Jesus his crutch. That's the Christmas present we should all bring to the manger: our crutches, our way of making God responsible for all the thinking and doing that we should be undertaking on our own. God provides minimum protection, but maximum support— support to help us grow up, to stretch our minds and hearts until they are as wide as God's universe. God doesn't want us narrow-minded, priggish, and subservient, but joyful and loving; as free for one another as God's love is freely poured out for us at Christmas in that babe in the manger.

# 2. Authority, Not Power

Readings: 1 Kings: 8–14
Luke 3: 1–15

Advent is the season of the Church that hails the coming of the Prince of Peace. At this time of the year in American history, we also observe the anniversary of the attack on Pearl Harbor, an event which took place on a Sunday, and which inevitably led the United States to war. The advent of the Prince of Peace and the attack on Pearl Harbor recall the contrast often made these days between authority and power. The word "power" has overtones of "naked," suggesting coercion, the use of force in some physical or psychological form. Authority, on the other hand, with its overtones of "legitimate," reflects qualities worthy of admiration. A person earns authority by showing understanding, wisdom, compassion. Generally, authority and power are both present to some degree in powerful individuals and institutions; but surely the ideal for people and institutions of power is to embody the attributes of authority.

Consider again how totally without power is the Prince of Peace, as he is about to enter the world. He whom we will hail as King of Kings and Lord of Lords will be born in a manger. He who is to be the bread of life for human beings is laid in the feed box of animals. The manger—like the cross—is a perfect symbol of powerlessness. Yet the fact that those in power will seek to destroy the child reflects an early recognition of the threat that authority always poses to power.

Even more arresting is this: By the end of his life, Jesus has certainly gained spiritual power over his disciples. But he refuses to exercise it. Judas is known to be a defector, but no action is taken. Peter three times denies his Lord, hardly the action of a cowed fanatic of the kind that followed Reverend Jim Jones to his death. In fact, would it not be fair to suggest that Jesus throughout his life will be authority incarnate, saying "No" to power in all its dehumanizing forms?

Is this the way God always deals with human beings— purely through authority, never through power? Let's go back to the first sentence of the New Testament lesson: "In the fifteenth year of Tiberius Caesar's reign" (there's imperial rank and power for you!) "when Pontius Pilate was governor of Judea" (again power) "Herod tetrarch of Galilee, his brother Philip tetrarch of the lands of Ituraea and Trachonitis, Lysanius tetrarch of Abilene" (power upon power!) "during the pontificate of Annas and Caiaphas" (religious power now added to secular power) "the word of God came to John son of Zechariah, *in the wilderness*" (Luke 3:1–2).

And how did the Word of God come to John the Baptist? We don't know, we're not told. What we do know is that in the Old Testament God frequently did manifest himself in power: to Moses in a burning bush; to many a Psalmist "He did fly upon the wings of the wind" (Ps. 18:10); to others he was in the earthquake—"The earth shook and trembled, the foundations also of the hills because of his wrath" (Ps. 18:7). We know that from the earliest of times and to the loftiest of prophets—at least to their imaginations—God did manifest himself in physical power.

But countering this idea is another in the Bible, one found perhaps for the first time in the story of Elijah. Here we read that God who laid the foundations of the earth, who keeps the stars in their courses—this same God speaks to the human soul in a still, small voice, beside whose authority the power of storm and earthquake is as nothing.

The stories of Elijah and John the Baptist show that those furthest from the seat of power are often nearer to the heart of things: "Power tends to corrupt," wrote Lord Acton, "and absolute power tends to corrupt absolutely." Centuries earlier, Rabbi Nahman of Bratislav said much the same: "Victory cannot tolerate truth, and if that which is true is spread before your very eyes, you will reject it, because you are a victor. Whoever would have truth itself must drive hence the spirit of victory; only then may he prepare to behold the truth."

The stories of Elijah and John the Baptist show that integrity springs from authority, not from power. The same can be said of courage. Those men of power, the Pharisees, must have been outraged to be called a "brood of vipers." But the multitudes, when they heard it, must have loved John for the enemies he dared to make. Because he himself was fearless, they must have felt protected by him. His courage must have been contagious; they must have begun to sense that there was little they couldn't do, once they saw in him that there was nothing they need fear.

And the story of Elijah shows, in the words of Athanasius: "The road to God is in the soul of every human being."

This Advent, in this of all seasons, dear Christians, let us not seek our salvation in the trappings of power. I know how authority and power vie in your souls, for they continually compete in mine. They vie in our role as parents, in the way we conduct ourselves on the job, in the way we perceive our beloved nation. And it is in the divorce of power from authority that we can trace the darkness in our personal lives and in the life of our nation.

Therefore let us allow God to search for us, as God did for Elijah, and to find us, as God found Elijah, there in the depths of our souls where we can distinguish true authority from illusory power. There, to the still, small voice of God, we can answer with our own: "Whom in heaven have I but thee? And there is none upon earth that I desire beside thee."

In this Advent time may the word of God, which came to John, come also to you. In this season of birth and rebirth, may the Word that calls forth shoots from dead stumps, a people from dry bones, sons and daughters from the stones at

our feet, babies from barren wombs, and life from the tomb—
may this Word, mightier than any power, call forth from you
a new creation.

# 3. Christ's Plan

Readings:   Isaiah 35:1–10
            Matthew 11:2–11

It was inevitable: John, who couldn't see evil without confronting it, and who therefore called to task no less a figure than King Herod himself for first seducing and then marrying his own sister-in-law—John the Baptist now sits in Herod's dungeons. He who lived with his face to the winds and with the sky as his roof, is now confined to four underground walls. The eagle of Israel is caged. Then, from prison, through his disciples, John sends to Jesus a question so full of poignancy as to break your heart: "Are you the one who is to come, or shall we look for another?" (Matt. 11:3).

Remember, it was only a short time before that John himself had baptized Jesus in the river Jordan, proclaiming to the crowd lining the bank that the long-awaited Messiah had come. But now the tide has turned against John and God's justice, the cause to which he had committed himself with an ardor rarely matched. So into John's heart crept those same doubts that afflict us in similar moments when nothing seems to be going our way. If you yourself have ever been jailed without cause, or robbed or raped, or have lost a loved one all too early, or a job or reputation unfairly, haven't you, too, thought of looking for a Messiah other than Jesus? And if you are a young mother or father, don't you sometimes doubt the efficacy of Christ's salvation, when national arrogance and cosmic foolishness seem intent upon dooming not only your newborn child, but every baby the world around?

It is possible, of course, that John asked his poignant question not to allay his own fears, but to lay to rest the doubts of his disciples who would be there to hear Jesus' answer. But it is probable that having predicted "the wrath to come" (Matt. 3:7), having claimed that "the axe is laid to the root of the trees" (Matt. 3:10), John, the prophet of cleansing judgment, was beginning to experience the darkness of impatience that always threatens to quench the light of compassion.

According to a Mormon myth, at Creation's start Christ and Satan were each requested to submit to God a plan for dealing with the infant human race that already was showing signs of delinquency. Satan's plan was simple (the kind that secretaries of state and defense frequently come up with): God has armies of angels at his command; why not assign an angel with punitive power to each human being? That should keep the race in line, and things moving along nicely.

In other words, Satan was the first "hard-liner," urging upon God the virtues of force. And isn't that what we all do? When things go badly for us personally—or nationally—don't we expect God, rather than ourselves, to straighten out the mess? Shouldn't God at the very least keep our children safe and sound, no matter how fast they drive; and shouldn't God keep the human race from annihilating itself, no matter what fiendish weapons we invent and insist on deploying? If ultimately children and the human race can only be saved by force, then so be it, by force—"But save us, God."

In contrast to Satan's, Christ's plan was extraordinarily imaginative, and implied a regard for humanity so high that Satan must have mocked it. "Let them have free will and go their own way," Christ proposed to God, "only let me live and die as one of them, both as an example of how to live, and to show them how much you care for them. The only answer to their delinquency is for them to realize that there is more mercy in you than sin in them."

At Christmas it becomes clear which plan God chose to implement. But if John the Baptist, confined to his cell, had a hard time understanding and accepting Christ's plan for salvation; if Christ himself, who submitted the plan, when nailed to the cross could not suppress his own doubts—"My God, my God, why hast thou forsaken me?"—it would surely be silly of us to think it easy to believe that a babe in a manger is all it takes to save our souls and the human race.

Let us turn now to Jesus' answer to John's question. Notice first of all, that when Jesus hears, "Are you the one who is to come, or shall we look for another?" he doesn't become the least bit defensive, as I certainly would have become. I guess that shows what extraordinary personal security there is in allowing God, and God alone, to provide you your identity. Jesus says simply, and with confidence, "Go and tell John what you see and hear" (11:4). Notice he does not say, "Tell John what I am saying. Here, take him a few copies of some recent sermons of mine, and some resolutions I've drafted on a variety of important subjects." (Christ would not be pleased with "resolutionary" Christianity.) No, Christ says, "Go and tell John what you see and hear"—in other words, what's happening.

And what is happening? "The blind receive their sight and the lame walk, lepers are cleansed and the deaf hear, and the dead are raised up, and the poor have good news preached to them" (11:5). All these things are not only literally, but better yet, figuratively, spiritually, and eternally true. Christ is fulfilling the promise of Isaiah: "Then the eyes of the blind shall be opened, and the ears of the deaf unstopped; then shall the lame leap like a hart, and the tongues of the dumb sing for joy" (35:5-6).

And the promise is for all time. But for this spiritual healing to take place today, as in the days when Christ walked on earth, we have to acknowledge that we have grossly misused the freedom of will that was central in Christ's plan to God. We have been blind to unpleasant truths about ourselves, deaf to the cries of the needy—if not at hand then far off, and occasionally as paralyzed by choices as was the proverbial medieval donkey placed equidistant from two bales of hay. We have to admit, as St. Paul did, that "we have sinned and fallen short" (Rom. 3:23). For evil is not guilt, as so many amateur psychiatrists pretend, but rather the effort to escape it. Evil is the human soul hiding from itself. Evil is pretending that whatever cars and weapons human beings make, God is responsible for their use. Evil is the soul of a nation explaining away its flaws by blaming others. Evil is the kind of self-protectiveness that invariably sacrifices others rather than ourselves. When, for example, Cain refused to acknowledge his imperfection, it was inevitable that he would seek to wreak havoc on the lives of others. In defense of their self-image, nations do this to such an extent that Albert Camus was led to name "legalized murder" the chief characteristic of our century.

And one more thing: If evil is a soul hiding from itself, if the primary motive of evil is disguise, we should not be surprised to find evil people in the churches. For what better way to disguise one's evil, from oneself and from others, than to attempt to wrap it all up in piety and to become a highly visible Christian—a preacher, let's say, or a deacon or a trustee? (No wonder St. Augustine said: "There are as many wolves within the fold as there are sheep without.")

"Only let me live and die as one of them, both as an example of how to live, and to show them that there is more mercy in you than sin in them." The world really divides itself between those held in the embrace of God's love who know it, and those so held who do not know it yet. Newton's hymn is so right:

> Amazing grace, how sweet the sound
> That saved a wretch like me.
> I once was lost, but now am found,
> Was blind, but now I see.

Now I see that God's love does not seek value, it creates it. Now I see that my identity is a gift from God, not an achievement of my own. Now I see that I don't have to prove myself, for God has taken care of that; all I have to do is to express myself in deeds of love and gratitude. Because I am held in the embrace of God's love, I can't run away—nor do I want to. How much better to face it all—the imperfections of my soul and my nation. In my hard moments I shall always be tempted, as was John, to seek a new messiah; but I shall pray God to deliver me from the temptation. For now I see that human freedom is the sole precondition for love, and that force can only contain evil, not destroy it. Forgiveness alone has that power. And if the abyss of love is deeper than the abyss of death, what shall we fear—our own death, the death of our children, or our husbands, wives, friends, even the death of the world? No, we need fear none of these, although God knows we must do all in our power to prevent every death we can.

Perhaps the most realistic hope for our time was voiced by Israel's Abba Eban: "People and nations do act wisely after they have exhausted all possible alternatives." I submit to you this Advent, that we have exhausted all possible alternatives. It's time now for Christmas, for Christ's plan. "Let them have their will and go their way, only let me live and die as one of them, both as an example of how to live and to show them how much you care for them." Come, Lord Jesus, come.

# 4. The Christmas Story

Reading:   Luke 2:1–20

While all four gospels have Jesus as their subject, each of them presents a distinct portrait of him. Of the four, the French philosopher Joseph Ernest Renan preferred St. Luke's, calling it: "the most beautiful book in the world." Why quarrel with such an estimate? The first two chapters of Luke contain three of the most beloved hymns of the church: Mary's "Magnificat," the "Nunc Dimittis" ("Lord, now lettest thou thy servant depart in peace"), and the chorus of the angels, the "Gloria in excelsis Deo." The last two chapters contain the three most treasured "words" from the cross: "Father, forgive them, for they know not what they do" (Luke 23:34); "Verily I say unto you, today thou shalt be with me in Paradise" (Luke 23:43); and "Father, into thy hands I commend my spirit" (Luke 23:46). And chapters 10 and 15 contain the two best-known parables: the Good Samaritan and the Return of the Prodigal Son. Furthermore, can you think of any pastoral narrative with "folk" poetry more lyrical than Luke's account of the birth of Jesus? Scholars will forever be trying to sort out the historically true from the eternally true, and trying to determine beyond any shadow of a doubt whether Luke was indeed the person tradition holds him to be—the Greek physician, traveling companion of St. Paul, and the author of the Book of Acts. That is the scholar's task. Ours, however, is different; ours, this Christmas morn, is to rescue the story from too much familiarity. So let's do a little Bible study.

"In those days a decree went out from Caesar Augustus that all the world should be enrolled" (Luke 2:1). Clearly, "all the world" is an exaggeration; for although Caesar Augustus was the great nephew of Julius Caesar, and was himself a great builder of roads and cities (of Rome it was said, "He found it brick, he left it marble."), still, even Caesar Augustus could enroll no more than the citizens of the empire. But stretching as it did in those days from the isle of Britain clear across Europe down to North Africa and eastward into Asia, the Roman Empire comprised almost the entire known world. So great was the wealth and power concentrated in Caesar Augustus that Romans considered him a god. To support his wealth and power, however, he needed troops and taxes. And so it was that every fourteen years a census was taken to see how much each citizen of the empire could pay, and to see who was liable for military conscription.

"And Joseph also went up from Galilee, from the city of Nazareth, to Judea, to the city of David, which is called Bethlehem . . . " (2:4). Jews, being fiercely nationalist, and believing as strongly as they did in their own God, were considered by the Romans too subversive to serve in the army. So it would appear that Joseph went to Bethlehem solely to enroll as a taxpayer. The journey from Nazareth to Bethlehem was eighty miles—long miles in those days, and arduous. Generally, people carried their own food, the inns providing only fodder for the animals and fires to cook over. When Joseph and Mary came to town, obviously nobody paid them any attention— even when, as it turned out, there was no room in the inn for a pregnant woman. The birth itself is recounted in all of one sentence: "And she gave birth to her firstborn son and wrapped him in swaddling cloths, and laid him in a manger, because there was no room for him in the inn" (2:7).

Had there been a Gallup poll in those days, there is no question that the mighty Emperor Caesar Augustus would have been voted a more significant figure than the babe born in a manger. Yet here we are, gathered once again to celebrate the birth of Jesus, while the Roman Empire is long vanished. Perhaps there's hope for the human race after all!

But that may be too rosy, too self-serving a statement. "There was no room for him in the inn," a phrase so descriptive really of all of Christ's life, may be as appropriate today as it was almost two thousand years ago. During Christ's time on earth, the only place where finally there was room for him was on the cross. Is there more room for him today in our over-crowded hearts, in our cities that say they can provide only temporary shelters for the homeless, in our nation where planning for nuclear war has become as American as apple pie? Maybe it would be more accurate to say that Christ's search for a place to be born, and our rejection of him—the search and the rejection both—go on today as they did then, and as they probably always will.

But let's continue with the story: "And there were in that same country shepherds abiding in the fields, keeping watch over their flocks by night" (2:8). I love the vagueness of it all. We don't know the exact grazing grounds of those sheep, nor for that matter, the exact spot where Jesus was born. It is as if God knew that one day there would be folk intent on commer-cializing every sacred spot in sight; it's as if he wanted to make sure that no one could ever claim that one spot on earth was nearer heaven than another. Likewise, no one can ever claim that one date is more sacred than another, for we don't know the exact day on which Christ was born. Some scholars reckon it was in the spring, because an efficient government, like the ancient Roman one, would not have insisted that peo-ple travel in midwinter to be enrolled. This conclusion is sup-ported by the fact that the shepherds were "keeping watch over their flock by night." Shepherds only stay up all night when there are lots of lambs to protect—that is, in spring. "Then why," we can ask, "was December 25th chosen?" The answer is, that like lambs, Christians were vulnerable in the first century. So it made sense for them to choose as their holiday the one that celebrated the birth of Rome, a day when Romans drank so much wine that none would notice the little bands of Christians having their own celebration.

But all this is only educated guesswork. More interesting than "Why the date?" or "Why the place?" is "Why the shepherds?" Why should shepherds have been the first disciples? Could it have been that, as in all times and places, God wanted all lives to be considered equally close to him? Shepherds were not only poor and powerless, in those days they were actually despised by Orthodox Jews, since, far out in the wilderness, they were unable to wash regularly and observe other ceremonial laws. Yet people needed them, particularly the Temple authorities, who, according to their laws, twice a day had to sacrifice to God an unblemished lamb. These authorities actually owned herds of sheep, and with the herds went the shepherds. It's a nice touch that those who looked after the sacrificial Temple lambs should have been the first to see the true Lamb of God, who "taketh away the sins of the world" (John 1:29).

And here's another nice touch: "And suddenly there was with the angels a multitude of the heavenly host praising God and saying, 'Glory to God in the highest, and on earth peace, goodwill towards men' " (or, as in a newer translation, "and on earth peace among those with whom God is pleased") (2:13–14). Whenever a child was born in ancient Palestine, it was customary for local musicians to gather at the child's house to sing God's praises. When Jesus was born, no Bethlehem musicians heard the news, so heavenly musicians had to take over. The first acclamations came from the sky itself— a host of angels singing, "Gloria in excelsis Deo."

And when the angels went away, what did the shepherds do? Did they sit around nursing their doubts, debating the "pros" and "cons" of going to Bethlehem? No, they acted immediately. Maybe that's another reason why the revelation came to them—they were ready. Their hearts were as high as the mountains among which they wandered, those peaks that are always the first to receive the dawn's early light.

But here's what impresses me most: When the shepherds found the babe "wrapped in swaddling cloths" (square cloths with a long bandage-like strip on one corner to wrap the cloth around the baby), when they found the babe "lying in a manger" (probably in a cave adjacent to the inn) did the humble scene shatter their hopes, destroy their faith? No, they understood what so few of us two thousand years later understand: that greater than Caesar Augustus, the man worshiped as a god, was their God become man. Better than all the armies of Caesar, this Lamb of God could bring peace. No longer would a divided, hostile, sinful world have to seek to appease a just god through the sacrifice of lambs: for their God, the just and merciful, "was in Christ reconciling the world to himself" (2 Cor. 5:19). Intuitively, the shepherds understood that "God so loved the world that he gave his only begotten son, that whosoever should believe in him would not perish but have everlasting life" (John 3:16).

Do you believe that? Is it too hard to believe, or too good to believe, we being strangers to such goodness? In any case, it's the Christmas message. So, like Mary, let us keep these things and ponder them in our hearts. Better yet, let's make room in these overcrowded hearts and cities of ours, that the Christ child may be born in us today. If we do, of this we may be certain: Our hearts will sing glorias not once, as did the angel chorus, but for ever, and ever, and ever.

# 5. The Story of the Magi

Readings: Isaiah 60:1–6
Matthew 2:1–12

Matthew's story of the visitors from the East who came seeking Jesus raises a lot of questions that can't be answered. Were they wise men or were they kings, these magi from the East? And who was it—seeing it wasn't Matthew—who decided their number was three, and called them Caspar, Melchior, and Balthazar? Moreover, since Matthew is the only one of the four Gospel writers to record their journey, how sure can we be that it actually took place? Perhaps the sole truly important question is the last, and the answer to it goes something like, "We cannot be sure that the journey actually took place. But the value of the story seems hardly to depend on its historical accuracy, inasmuch as the story doesn't so much enthrone the Christ-child as the child enthrones the story."

I think it helps to see the story as a small masterpiece presented to Jesus by his disciple, the erstwhile tax-collector, who, in following Jesus, left everything behind except his quill. Think of the truths Matthew manages to express in twelve short verses: the truth that people come from afar and by many ways to worship Christ; the truth that no place is too lowly to kneel in; the truth that as knowledge grows, so too must reverence and love, else doubts will paralyze the mind and much learning dry the heart. And what truth is symbolized in that star over Bethlehem, God's sign set high in the mystery of the night sky? Doesn't its light beckon to our deepest longing, which finally is not for mother or father, grocer or lover, but for a savior—a longing that can be answered only from beyond our earth? And yet a sign is only that—a sign, and the choice remains ours to journey towards it or to stay stuck wherever we are.

Actually, that last truth comes through powerfully in the story. Although they lived only six miles north of Bethlehem, Herod and "all Jersualem" (as Matthew refers to the urbane Jerusalemites who surrounded the King) never even saw the star until the strangers from distant lands pointed it out to them. Were they too much in love with and blinded by their candles and torches to see the heavenly light? To paraphrase Thoreau, for every three farseeing, truly wise persons, there are hundreds who can't see beyond their noses. They are clever, perhaps, but not wise.

And what was the reaction of these hundreds of Jerusalemites to the announcement of the birth of the new child? Hostility: "Herod the King was troubled, and all Jerusalem as well" (2:3). The last thing in the world most luxury-ridden, power-hungry people want (although it is the one thing they really need) is a savior to save them from the corruption of wealth and power. Among sinful people, the most common reaction to moral evaluation is always violence. Recall Herodias, wife of Herod, who demanded the head of her moral evaluator, John the Baptist. Recall that anti-semites hate Jews not because they were Christ-slayers but because they were Christ-bearers.

No more surprising than such hostility, although more disappointing, was the apparent indifference of the chief priests and scribes. You would have thought that they would be excited at the fulfillment of the prophecy they all knew so well; that they would have leapt at the chance to join the wise men on the last leg of their journey—all of six miles. Instead, they apparently went back to their books, preferring their faith *in vitro* (under glass) rather than *in vivo* (in life).

Today, the same three fundamental choices face all of us: With Herod and the urbane Jerusalemites, we can choose to be hostile to Christ; with the chief priests and scribes, we can choose to be indifferent to him (say, by being devoted to church work, but not the work of the church!); or, with the wise men, we can choose to fall on our knees and worship, offering Christ our hearts' best treasures.

I think the adoration scene itself becomes even more powerful if, following a later tradition that linked back to Isaiah's prophecy—"And nations shall come to thy light, and kings to the brightness of thy rising" (Isa. 60:3)—we now choose to see the wise men as kings: Caspar representing Europe, Melchior Asia, and Balthazar Africa. Picture three kings with crowns on their heads and rings on their fingers, surrounded by servants with torches to lead them through the night. Picture them on horseback, old Caspar on a gentle mare; young, black Balthazar riding a steed as white as snow. Picture three kings with all their worldly power, yet graced with the wisdom of heaven, able to see more beauty in a manger than in Herod's splendid palace, more love in that child than in the hearts of "all Jerusalem." Picture three wise kings who see around the child the shadows of death, but within him the light of life.

And what symbolism there is in their gifts of gold, frankincense and myrrh! Gold, of course, represents our worldly substance, our household and national budgets, which cry out these days as much as ever to be dedicated to Christ. Look carefully at almost any of your much-heralded economic recoveries, and you will see that accompanying it is an ever-widening gap between rich and poor. And how dedicated to Christ are the millions of dollars we Americans send abroad to prop up corrupt and murderous governments?

Frankincense has come to symbolize our innermost thoughts —which, of course, need also to be dedicated to the Christchild. University professors often talk of the "pursuit of truth" as if truth were something evasive, like a rabbit; whereas much of the time it is we who are evasive, dodging and hiding from the unpleasant personal and national exposure the truth often brings. Certainly the truth we see in Christ is one that searches for us, seeking to deepen our awareness of God and life, seeking to redirect our thoughts from selfish interests toward God and our neighbors.

Finally, because it is used in embalming, myrrh has come

to stand for our sorrow and suffering, the hardest things, perhaps, to dedicate to Christ. When we lose someone or something near and dear to us—a child through death, a spouse through divorce, or a long and happily held job—we often turn away from God, thinking God has deserted us; whereas, in fact, God's heart is probably as broken as our own. These moments reveal something harsh but important for us to grasp, namely, that we have been using God to realize our own ambitions—good ambitions, perhaps, but ours nonetheless—instead of allowing God to fulfill her ambitions through us. If God can use our money, if God can use our innermost thoughts, how much more can God do with our suffering and sorrow? And of course, in handing over our broken hearts to God lies our best hope for their healing.

Dearly beloved, beginning on this Epiphany Sunday and continuing throughout the year that follows, I pray that all the promise, hope, love, and joy of the Christmas season may accompany you until once again we gather to celebrate the birth of the Christ-child.

# 6. Some Thoughts on Martin Luther King, Jr.'s, Birthday

"Let not the foreigner who has joined himself to the Lord say: 'The Lord will surely separate me from his people' . . . Thus says the Lord God, who gathers the outcasts of Israel, 'I will gather yet others to him besides those already gathered' " (Isa. 56:10).

"There is neither Jew nor Greek, there is neither bond nor free, there is neither male or female, for you are all one in Christ Jesus" (Gal. 3:28).

And to these words of Isaiah and Paul, let us add these: "Procrastination is still the thief of time. Life often leaves us standing bare, naked and dejected with a lost opportunity . . . Over the bleached bones and jumbled residue of numerous civilizations are writ the pathetic words: 'Too late' . . . We still have a choice today: non-violent co-existence or violent co-annihilation. We must move past indecision to action."

The author of those last words, from *Where Do We Go From Here*, died before he was forty. Yet Marthin Luther King, Jr.'s, prophetic life and martyr's death changed all who knew him, and millions more who only heard, saw or read about him. Indeed, we can say that until the very end of American history this nation will never again be the same because of him.

Somewhere I read of a farmer who, after his conversion to Christ, cried out, "Even my chickens know I'm different." That's a rare kind of conversion. If truth be told, most Christians would rather enshrine than follow Christ. The same holds for prophets such as Martin Luther King, Jr. And well I remember, when that great man Pope John XXIII died, how eagerly

Protestants joined the throngs saying, "This is the one person the world can least afford to lose." Yet saying that in no way affected their basic anti-Catholicism. Never mind that he was only the pope!

There are good reasons for all this. What the prophets teach us to believe and what the world rewards as belief are never the same. Martin preached that gentleness takes no more courage than violence. How many in the world are ready to be that courageous? Martin preached that compassion is more valuable than any ideology. Tell that to a Cambodian Communist, or to a Latin American anti-Communist. Martin preached that we should be governed by our dreams, not our fears. The largest peacetime build-up of military power in the history of the planet belies that belief. What then shall we say? That we love our martyrs only after we have slain them as prophets?

"Thus says the Lord God, who gathers the outcasts of Israel, 'I will gather yet others to him besides those already gathered' " (Isa. 56:8). Prophets recognize that there is a progressive nature to moral judgment. So they criticize what is in terms of what might be. They judge the darkness of the present by the light of the future. And they reject what is narrow and provincial in the name of what is universal. Prophets know that just as all rivers meet in the sea, so all individuals, races, and nations meet in God. "There is neither Jew nor Gentile, there is neither bond nor free, there is neither male nor female; for you are all one in Christ Jesus."

In a memorable moment in Herman Wouk's *War and Remembrance*, a saga of World War II, Captain Henry, a U.S. naval officer, is brought into a bullet-ridden building in Stalingrad. Behind a plank desk sits a tough-looking grey-headed man in uniform, his face lined with fatigue. He doesn't look friendly. It is 1943 and more and more Soviets are beginning to be convinced that the British and Americans are prepared to fight to the last Russian, that they are never going to open up a second front in Europe. For their part, the British and Americans are leery lest the Russians, exhausted by the war, revert to their former truce with Hitler and make a separate peace with the Germans, as they had in World War I. So the American too is reserved. Behind the desk the Soviet official raises thick eyebrows at his compatriot, General Yevlenko, who has brought this man to Stalingrad. In response, Yevlenko puts the one remaining hand that a German explosive has left him— puts this good hand on the shoulder of the American and says, "Nash"—"Ours"—and in an instant the word has worked magic. Suspicion on both sides is erased.

How many human problems would resolve, or rather, dissolve themselves if all those who are in reality one in God, would put a hand on one another's shoulder and say "ours." I have in mind not only Russians and Americans, but blacks and whites, here and in South Africa; Arabs and Jews in the Middle East and women and men everywhere. It is precisely to that kind of practical Utopia that we have here to rededicate ourselves if we are properly to honor him who said, "We still have a choice today: non-violent co-existence or violent co-annihilation. We must move past indecision to action."

"Through many a danger, toil, and snare (we) have already come." Progress has been made since the 1960s, because that was a decade of ethical unrest. Dr. King would be pleased that in the ten years from 1966 to 1976 black enrollment in colleges increased 275 percent, from 282,000 to 1,062,000. In 1976, 11 percent of all collegians were black as opposed to 4.5 percent in 1966. And when they graduated, few of those students went back to the streets from which so many came—the streets of Harlem, Bedford-Stuyvesant, Roxbury, East Detroit, Watts. And in fairness to whites, these college-educated blacks met more curiosity than hostility in the neighborhoods and jobs they integrated.

As blacks are breaking up all-white patterns, so women are upsetting the patriarchal structures of America. And this bodes well for the gay liberation movement, as historically only societies that subordinate women are harsh in their treatment of homosexuality. (In *The Courage to Love*, I've dealt with the gross misinterpretations of Scripture on the part of those who, for their convenience, forget that the Nazis put over 200,000 homosexuals to death.)

But what of those streets in Harlem, Bedford-Stuyvesant, Roxbury, East Detroit, St. Louis, and Watts? Who today puts a friendly hand on the shoulders of those teenagers? Are they "ours" or do they prove that class is a tougher nut to crack than race? And isn't the arms race outstripping the process of arms control? Aren't we then ourselves in danger of honoring King as a martyr, while trampling on what he stood for as a prophet, as long as we fail to say "ours" to the poor and the foreigner? And King himself made the connection: "A nation that continues year after year to spend more money on military defense than on programs of social uplift is approaching spiritual death."

Today we are far nearer that death, and it is time for Christians who would honor their fallen prophet to take note. The church is called to be the Bride of Christ, not the whore of Babylon. She cannot bind herself to the Prince of Peace and go awhoring after the gods of war. She cannot proclaim the Gospel of Christ while officiating at the altars of anticommunism. She cannot stand for peace while lying prostrate before the shrine of "national security." If she is to be the church, then she must stand against militarism, proclaiming that there is no security in arms alone; that in fact, ironically, the more destructive our weapons the more vulnerable and insecure we all become.

I cannot help recalling that Martin Luther King, Jr. chose the pulpit of Riverside Church to denounce the war in Vietnam. That same night, also in opposition to President Johnson, he declared that the choice was between guns and butter. He got roasted, not only by government officials, but other civil rights leaders as well, and by *The New York Times*. But he was right. His, that night, was one of the great prophetic speeches of American history.

It was King's compassion that led him consistently to make

common cause with sufferers. And it was King's genius to be able to take a Christian message out of the sanctuary of a church and into the corridors of power. Remember, he was leading a poor people's march on Washington when he was assassinated.

Something like that needs to be undertaken again. Let us think hard about this prophet and martyr who said we should be governed by our dreams, more than our fears; who said that compassion was more valuable than any ideology; who could lay a hand on anyone's shoulder and say "ours" because he knew that the Lord "will gather yet others to him besides those already gathered." More than any other human being I ever met, Martin knew that "there is neither Jew nor Greek, there is neither bond nor free, there is neither male nor female; for (we) are all one in Christ Jesus." Amen.

# 7. One Blood, Many Nations

Reading: John 8:2–11

On this day, designated in many churches "International" Sunday, it is fitting that the sermon text should be St. Paul's ringing proclamation to the Athenians: "God has made of one blood all the nations of the earth" (Acts 17:26).

I like the "blood" metaphor; for, when you stop to think of it, each of our bodies is a revelation of the inclusive community Paul proclaims. As the theologian James M. Nelson writes in his book *Between Two Gardens*:

Each of us is made up of more than a trillion individual cells, all attempting to work together and maintain one another. Our bodies are communities with their own ventilation systems, sewage systems, communication systems, heating units, and a billion miles of inter-connecting streets and alleys.

Our bodies are not only communities in themselves but, even more, communities in relationship with the earth. Our bodily fluids carry the same chemicals as the primeval seas . . . Our bones contain the sugar that once flowed in the sap of now-fossilized trees. The nitrogen which binds our bones together is the same as that which binds nitrates to the soil.

Likewise, at their best, music, art, and literature proclaim our human oneness. What could be more quintessentially British and at the same time more universal than *King Lear*? What could be more quintessentially German and at the same time more universally understood than the cry of Goethe's Faust: "*Augenblick, verweile doch, du bist so schon*" ("Moment, ah still delay, thou art so fair")? What could be more quintessentially Spanish and at the same time more universally needed than the benediction given each of us by Unamuno at the end of his book *The Tragic Sense of Life*: "May God deny you peace but give you glory" ("*Y Diós no te dé paz y sí gloria*")?

And of the experience of tragedy, is it not true that when cancer eats at our vitals, when our bones become brittle and break, when genetic diseases deform innocent infants—is it not true that there is still revelation in the knowledge that this was not the way it was meant to be? Be the tragedy that of illness or of racial prejudice, be it the abuse of women and children, or the terror of war, tragedy always derives its meaning from a vision of unity and harmony. Such is the testimony of the body and the body politic to God's peace—his *shalom*—in the age to come, when "nation shall not lift up sword against nation" (Mic. 4:3), when "the world shall be full of the knowledge of the Lord as the waters cover the sea" (Isa. 11:9).

"God has made of one blood all the nations of the earth." Black, white, yellow, red, smart and stupid, starved and stuffed, from nations large and small, whatever our creed, we all belong one to another. That's the way God made us. Christ died to keep us that way. Our sin is only and always that we are trying to put asunder what God herself has joined together.

Why *do* we? Why do the nations—as Scripture puts it—"so furiously rage together" (Ps. 2:1), resisting their God-given unity? The historian Herbert Butterfield gave perhaps the central reason when he wrote: "In the kind of world that I see in history, there is one sin that locks people up in all their other sins, and fastens people and nations more tightly than ever in their predicaments, namely the *sin of self-righteousness*." Certainly it affects all nations, albeit in diverse ways. The Swiss, for example, are inordinately proud of their neutrality—and quite pleased with the money it has made them. The French still believe in their *mission civilatrice*—which often was accompanied by the Foreign Legion and today seems to include *la force frappe nucleáire*. For awhile, in the 1940s, the Germans considered themselves supermen; and in the 1960s, Ghana, under Nkrumah, thought its solutions were the answer to almost all African problems. The Chinese and Indians are prone to feel that the age their civilizations boast gives them a corner on the world market for wisdom; while the British, the British, well—

> In the beginning, by some mistake,
> Men were foreigners all created,
> Till heaven conceived a nobler plan
> And there was born an Englishman.
> Conceive the difference, if you can,
> Had Adam been an Englishman.

And, there is something in the American mind that perennially returns to the thought that of all the nations on the face of the earth, God smiles the most on ours.

We Americans are the peculiar chosen people—the Israel of our time; we bear the ark of the liberties of the world. . . . Long enough have we been skeptics with regard to ourselves, and doubted whether, indeed, the political Messiah had come. But he has come in *us*, if we would but give utterance to his promptings.

So wrote Herman Melville in *White Jacket*. Nor did the idea of America as God's political Messiah die with the last century. At the beginning of this one, Senator Albert J. Beveridge proclaimed to his colleagues that "God . . . has marked the American people to finally lead in the redemption of the world. This is the divine mission of America. . . . We are the trustees of the world's progress, guardians of its righteous peace." Not long thereafter, President Wilson assured the citizens of Cheyenne, Wyoming, that "America had the infinite privilege of fulfilling her destiny and saving the world." Some of us remember, more recently, President Nixon's insistence during the war in Vietnam that "our beliefs must be combined with a crusading zeal, not just to hold our own but to change the world . . . and to win the battle for freedom." And (in his 1984 State of the Union address), after announcing his fourth great goal—a meaningful and lasting peace—President Reagan declared, "It is our highest aspiration. And our record is clear: Americans resort to force only when we must. We have never been aggressors. We have always struggled to defend freedom and democracy." (Tell that to Native Americans and blacks, to the Mexicans, to the Nicaraguans, in whose country the Marines have landed no less than fourteen times, to the Filipinos and Puerto Ricans, the Salvadorans, the black South Africans!)

In any nation, self-righteousness is anathema to God and disastrous to human unity, because it concentrates all attention on the sins of others. It is deaf to St. Augustine's admonition: "Never fight evil as if it were something that arose totally outside of yourself." Moreover, self-righteousness tends toward zealotry—which, by providing a nation with motives that appear to it selfless, can lead in turn to the preparation of a kind of "redemptive" violence. Recall abolitionist John Brown and his favorite line: "Without the shedding of blood there is no remission of sins." Recall again the State of the Union address, whose most riveting moment had to be when President Reagan presented to the Congress a Marine sergeant, and every congressman in view of the TV camera stood up to applaud the hero—as if the whole world had not sat on its hands and watched in horror this latest example of American redemptive violence, our invasion of Grenada.

The clear and present danger today is not that we will be overcome and overrun by Communists, but that we Americans will become like the exultant Pharisees, who were prepared to stone to death the woman caught in adultery. Interestingly enough, in this case, Jesus does not dispute the sin, nor the punishment of death, nor even the condemnation of only the woman, when quite obviously it takes more than one person to be caught in the act of adultery. No, Jesus simply questions the right of anyone who is himself guilty to pass judgment on another; "Let him who is without sin among you cast the first stone" (John 8:7). He takes an example of conspicuous wrongdoing and uses it not to nourish self-righteousness, but rather to heighten awareness of the sin common to all human beings, and of the need we all share for repentance.

In repentance lies our hope, the hope that we can see the crisis today before it is validated by disaster tomorrow. Were we Americans to repent of the self-righteousness that fastens us in our predicament, we would realize that if we are not yet one with the Soviets in love, at least we are one with them in sin—which is no mean bond, for it precludes the possibility of separation through judgment. That is the meaning of "Judge not, that ye be not judged" (Matt. 7:1). Were we to repent of our self-righteousness, the existence of Soviet missiles would remind us of nothing so much as our own; Soviet threats to rebellious Poles would call to mind American threats to the Sandinistas; Afghanistan would suggest Vietnam. Soviet suppression of civil liberties at home would remind us of our own complicity in the repression of these same civil liberties abroad—in the Philippines, in Pakistan, in Honduras, in South Africa. Were we to repent we would drop the insidious double standard: They arm, it's evil; we arm, it's for national security. We would cease the self-deluding practice of judging our own motives by our political intentions, and Soviet motives by their military capabilities.

Jesus would never be "soft on communism," any more than he would be soft on capitalism. But I can hear him saying, "Let the nation without sin among you aim the first missile." And given Christ's far-reaching mercy, I can hear him, at some future and blessed date, addressing a repentent Soviet Union and a repentant United States with words of assurance and admonition similar to the ones he offered that sad and lonely figure a long time ago: "Neither do I condemn you. Go and build nuclear weapons . . . no more."

"God has made of one blood all the nations of the world." So true is that unity, that our every effort to deny it only succeeds in making it all the more imperative. The present state of affairs is such that if we do not shortly become one in life, we'll all be one in death.

Four hundred years ago, Galileo looked into the telescope and saw that Copernicus was right: The earth is not the center of the universe, but only one modest planet revolving around its sun. Today anyone with 20/20 vision, and humility to match, can see that no one country—no matter how glorious its past, how brilliant its future, how mighty its arms, or how generous its people—no one country is at the center of this earth. Today, as eternally in the eyes of God, there is only one century, the human century. So on this International Sunday, let us pledge ourselves to bringing the vision of God's peaceable Kingdom into international fruition. Let us take to heart the words written so long ago:

Come let us go up to the mountain of Yahweh, to the house of the God of Jacob,

That he may teach us his ways and that we may walk in his paths.

For out of Zion shall go forth the law, and the word of the Lord out of Jerusalem.

He shall judge between the nations, and shall decide among many peoples;

And they shall beat their swords into ploughshares, and their spears into pruning hooks;

Nation shall not lift up sword against nation, neither shall they learn war any more (Mic. 4:2, 3).

# 8. Abraham Lincoln: Spiritual Center of America's History*

Reading:  Psalm 19

In that rare year when Lincoln's birthday falls on a Sunday, it seems right that in the United States sermons be given recalling the president who, more than any other, stands at the spiritual center of American history.

His official duty as president, Lincoln knew, was to preserve the Union; but his deepest personal wish was that all people everywhere might be free. In his youth he argued against slavery in the light of "self-evident truths," but in his later presidential years he fought it in terms of a biblical understanding of work. In *The Religion of Abraham Lincoln*, William Wolf records that to the Baptists of the Home Missionary Society, Lincoln wrote:

To read in the Bible, as the word of God himself, that "In the sweat of thy face thou shalt eat bread," and to preach therefrom that "In the sweat of other men's faces shalt thou eat bread," to my mind can scarcely be reconciled with honest sincerity. When brought to my final reckoning, may I have to answer for robbing no man of his goods; yet more tolerable even this, than of robbing one of himself, and all that he was. When, a year or two ago, those professedly holy men of the South, met in semblance of prayer and devotion, and, in the name of Him who said "As ye would all men should do unto you, do ye even so unto them," appealed to the Christian world to

---

* For the information about Lincoln in this Chapter I am grateful to William Wolf's book *The Religion of Abraham Lincoln* (New York: Seabury Press, 1963).

aid them in doing to a whole race of men, as they would have no man do unto themselves, to my thinking, they condemned and insulted God and His church, far more than did Satan when he tempted the Savior with the Kingdoms of the earth. The devil's attempt was no more false, and far less hypocritical. But let me forbear, remembering it is also written, "Judge not, lest ye be judged."

No American president has had a clearer vision of God's will and a more unself-righteous perspective on himself. No American president has been more attuned to the pain and the sorrow tearing at the life of his people. And no citizen of this country—and I bear in mind Jonathan Edwards and Reinhold Niebuhr—no citizen of this country has interpreted more eloquently this sorrow and this pain in the light of the great biblical motifs of judgment, punishment, justice, mercy, and reconciliation. (Let us remember, when we hear Lincoln referring to the Bible as he so frequently does, that the people of his day read the Bible far more than people do today, and that Lincoln never used the Bible except to be inclusive of all citizens.) Biblical judgment—"The sins of the fathers are visited upon the sons and unto their children's children" (Num. 14:15)—says that life is consequential, that we cannot escape history, that the world swings on an ethical hinge: Loosen that hinge, and all history and even nature will feel the shock; it says that individuals and nations do not so much break the Ten Commandments as they are broken upon them, for, in the words of Saint Paul, "God is not mocked" (Gal. 6:7). All this Abraham Lincoln knew better than most, and he said it without pomposity. Rather, he spoke with humor, which has much to do with the Christian faith; for while the faith takes care of the ultimate incongruities of life, humor does nicely with the intermediate ones. More than that: By helping to destroy the illusion of our control over life, humor opens us up to the realization of God's governance.

Like so many in the 1960s and early 1970s, I went time and again to Washington to protest the war in Vietnam. It was a duty, but not a pleasant one. And while these demonstrations were rightly viewed by many as an exercise in democracy, somehow they left me strangely depressed. To raise my spirits at day's end, I generally stole away for a few quiet moments at the Lincoln Memorial. I didn't know then that Lincoln's relationship to blacks was not quite what I hoped it was; nor did I know that he never really came to terms with his humble origins, that he was a bit of a social climber, a bit harsh on his father. But those shortcomings would not have mattered to me at that time. For I went to the Lincoln Memorial knowing that when he was in the House of Representatives Lincoln, too, had protested a war, the war against Mexico, describing it in terms that I felt were proper also for the war in Vietnam, as "unnecessary and unconstitutional"—and I knew that those words had cost him his congressional seat. And I went because of what I felt the Memorial itself conveys. Unlike many other American heroes commemorated in Washington, Lincoln is not pictured astride a rearing stallion. Unlike Jefferson, he's not even standing: He's sitting, for heaven's sake, sitting in an old armchair. Yet all the depth and grandeur are there, all the greatness that undoubtedly was his after he had grown from an average self-centered small-town politician—albeit one of unsuspected talents—to a statesman of world stature.

A story was told in Lincoln's time of a man who asked the pilot of a Mississippi riverboat how long he had been plying his trade.

"Twenty-six years," the pilot replied.

"Then," said the man, "you know where all the rocks are, all the shoals and sandbars."

"No," said the pilot. 'I just know where they ain't."

And that's where Lincoln consistently tried to steer our ship of state: out there in the deep waters, far from the sandbars of party sectarianism, the rocks of tribalistic chauvinism. That is why, in ending slavery, he was equally concerned for the slaveholders: "In giving freedom to the slave, we assure freedom to the free—honorable alike in what we give, and what we preserve." That is why, when the Civil War was drawing to a close, Lincoln came out so clearly for amnesty. Like any sensible man he feared anarchy on the one hand as he did despotism on the other, and his legal training enhanced his respect for the law. Yet he pushed hard against the legal limits when laws seemed to him unjust, and when wisdom, rooted in compassion, revealed to him that human relations are finally just that—human, not contractual. As "the Sabbath belongs to man, not man to the Sabbath" (Mark 2:27), so Lincoln understood the law to be a good servant, but a bad master. As a result, not a single soldier or officer who wore the gray— not even those like Robert E. Lee, who had once worn the blue—not a single confederate was punished for breaking the law of the land. Of the states that had seceded Lincoln said, "Finding them safely at home, it would be utterly immaterial whether they had ever been abroad."

His ability to pilot the ship of state safely in deep waters, to see big issues in a big way, was aided by an unrelenting willingness to question. I think it fair, and in a church important, to say that because Lincoln doubted the formulation of certain creeds and catechisms he became more deeply aware of the realities they were meant to represent. "Probably it is my lot," he wrote as a young man, "to go on in a twilight, feeling and reasoning my way through life, as questioning doubting Thomas did. But in my poor, maimed way, I bear with me, as I go on, a seeking spirit of desire for a faith that was with him of olden times, who, in his need, as I in mine, exclaimed, 'Help thou my unbelief.' "

Because he refused to be dogmatic, and because he knew how selfish human beings can be even as they claim to be the very opposite, Lincoln abhorred self-righteousness. After reading several dispatches from young General McClellan, all of which began, "Headquarters: in the saddle," Lincoln remarked to the members of his cabinet, "It's strange how the general keeps his headquarters where most people prefer to put their hindquarters." Even more trying than his generals was the self-righteousness of the clergy, who visited him in

droves. After the departure of a particularly obnoxious dele-
gation, Lincoln turned to an aide and told him the story of a
small boy who sculpted a beautiful church out of mud, a
church replete with pews and pulpit. When asked "Where's
the preacher?" the boy replied, "I ran out of mud."

For the most part, the clergy were pressing for an immediate
abolition of slavery in all the states and territories. But although he had detested slavery since childhood, Lincoln's dilemma was real: as president he had taken an oath of office to
uphold the Constitution, which provided for slavery, at least
in the original thirteen states. (Scholars question whether the
Emancipation Proclamation was in fact warranted by the Constitution, as Lincoln finally decided it was.) Because he was
willing to maintain tension, no matter how painful, Lincoln
was sensitive to the dilemmas of others, particularly the one
that tormented the Quakers. What were they to do, opposed
as they were to both war and oppression, when war seemed
to be the only way to abolish the oppression?

But although he questioned creedal formulations, and was
sharply aware both of the mixture of human motivations and
the complexities of history, Lincoln never for a moment doubted
the word of the psalmist that "the judgments of the Lord are
true and righteous altogether" (Ps. 19:9). He doubted whether
these judgments could be mechanistically applied from outside, as the clergy frequently suggested, but he was certain
that they would always be enacted organically within history,
for—once again—"God is not mocked."

To read the Lincoln-Douglas debates is to hear Lincoln ex-
pound American history as would a biblical prophet, the plumb
line being morality rooted in the righteous will of God. He
appreciates the dilemma faced by the founders of the Republic:
unity with slavery, or the abolition of slavery and no Republic—at least not one comprised of thirteen states. Choosing
unity, as they did, of course did not solve the dilemma, but
left a moral poison in the bloodstream of American life. By
prohibiting the extension of slavery to the Northwest Territo-

ries in the Ordinance of 1787, our forbears had at least put slavery, as Lincoln saw it, "in course of ultimate extinction," a principle, he argued, that had remained intact despite the Missouri Compromise of 1820, reaffirmed in 1850. But now Senator Douglas was proposing that "popular sovereignty"— the settlers themselves—should decide the question of slavery in Kansas and Nebraska. That, said Douglas, was the democratic way. Answered Lincoln, "This declared indifference, but as I must think covert real zeal for the spread of slavery, I cannot but hate. I hate it because of the monstrous injustice of slavery itself." As to the argument of self-government, he said,

If the negro is not a man, why in that case, he who is a man may as a matter of self-government, do just as he pleases with him. But if the negro is a man, is it not to that extent a total destruction of self-government, to say that he too shall not govern himself? When the white man governs himself, and also governs another man, that is more than self-government, that is despotism. . . . No man is good enough to govern another man, without that other's consent. I say this is the leading principle—the sheet anchor of American republicanism.

To guard against self-righteousness, Lincoln describes the problem as national rather than regional:

They [southern whites] are just what we would be in their situation. If slavery did not now exist amongst them, they would not introduce it. If it did exist amongst us, we would not instantly give it up. This I believe of the masses north and south.

Because in these debates Lincoln called forth "the better angels of our nature," at least in part for that reason, I like to think he was elected president.

Then came the Civil War, during which he promised, "I shall do nothing in malice. What I deal with is too vast for malicious dealing." The way he interpreted this horrendous event in the light of the great biblical motifs of judgment, punishment, justice, mercy, and reconciliation, confirms his place at the spiritual center of American history. You remember the Second Inaugural; quoting from Matthew 18, he says:

"Woe unto the world because of offenses! For it must needs be that offenses come; but woe to that man by whom the offense cometh!" If we shall suppose that American slavery is one of those offenses which, in the providence of God, must needs come, but which, having continued through His appointed time, He now wills to remove, and that He gives to both North and South, this terrible war, as the woe due to those by whom the offense came, shall we discern therein any departure from those divine attributes which the believers in a living God always ascribe to Him? Fondly do we hope—fervently do we pray—that this mighty scourge of war may speedily pass away. Yet, if God wills that it continue, until all the wealth piled by the bond-man's two hundred and fifty years of unrequited toil shall be sunk, and until every drop of blood drawn with the lash, shall be paid with another drawn with the sword, as was said three thousand years ago, so it must be said again "the judgments of the Lord are pure and righteous altogether."

With malice toward none; with charity for all; with firmness in the right, as God gives us to see the right, let us strive on to finish the work we are in; to bind up the nation's wounds; to care for him who shall have borne the battle, and for his widow, and his orphan—to do all which may achieve and cherish a just, and a lasting peace, among ourselves, and with all nations.

I hope Americans will take time today and in the days to come to think of the pain and sorrow still tearing at the life of our nation. The way we conduct ourselves at home and abroad indicates how far we have strayed from our spiritual center. But if America has lost her way, I feel confident she will find it again. Because we once elected a president who knew so clearly that he stood under the living God of history, I feel certain that the American people will one day again fit the description he gave us—"God's almost chosen people"—if only, like him, we would seek to build our national life on the bedrock of Scriptural faith.

# 9. Beating the Blues

A cheerful heart is a good medicine, but a downcast spirit dries up the bones. (Proverbs 17:22)

If it's true that at Christmas, and as recently as Epiphany, people were on tiptoes with expectation, by mid-February they are simply standing around, flat-foot, wondering if there is some purposeful direction for their feet to go. Yes, February is the time for the blues. The climate alone is enough to cool the cockles of the warmest heart. As opposed to June, life in February seems to throw more stones, and it's harder than usual to pick them up and build an altar! This is the time of year when children complain, "Why are all the vitamins in the spinach and not in the ice cream?" This is the time of year when their fathers and mothers recall G. B. Shaw's definition of love as "a gross exaggeration of the difference between one person and everybody else." Yes, it was at this time of year that a dilapidated old New Yorker crept out of the cold and into the warmth of a greasy spoon, there to be met by a big ugly waiter with a filthy apron.

"OK, Mac, what's yours?"

"Two fried eggs, and a few kind words!"

Soon the big ugly waiter returned, slapped the eggs down on the table, and started off.

"Hey, friend, you forgot the few kind words."

"Oh yeh . . . Don't eat dem eggs."

So what to do, when hope looks more like a candle about to burn out than a beacon blazing across the sky? What to do to beat the blues?

We could always pray for an encounter with God, an experience so overwhelming that it caused Moses to take off his shoes, Elijah to cover his face, Isaiah to fall apart and break into confession, and Peter to drop to his knees. But that might be to tempt the Lord; you can't, after all, order an encounter. Besides, even for prophets and saints such encounters are rare, which is probably for the best:

> Go, go, go said the bird,
> Humankind cannot bear very much reality.
> —T. S. Eliot, *Four Quartets*

What all of us *can* do, even in cities like New York, is to appreciate daily what the hymn "O worship the King" calls "the earth with its store of wonders untold." Living on the shores of the Hudson, I spend a fair amount of time observing gulls. Some of the time, mostly when they are in the water, fighting and hollering at each other, they only succeed in deepening my depression, reminding me of certain meetings I attend, and also of the origin of the expression "bird-brained." But they have only to take off into the air and start gliding, diving, hovering, and I find myself talking to their Creator and mine: "O God, if only we humans could be who we are so effortlessly."

"Thy bountiful care, what tongue can recite; it breathes in the air, it shines in the light." "The world," said Chesterton, "does not lack for wonders, only for a sense of wonder." Even human beings—nay, especially human beings—for all their gaucheries and downright wickedness, are wondrous. Of course, if your desire is to control them, human beings will appear smaller than they really are. But if you simply *wonder* at them— their sensibilities, subtleties, and surprises, human beings will appear bigger than life. I never cease wondering at the courage that persists amid the fury of disease and pain. I never cease wondering at the way the human spirit in this city survives insult and injury. My mind boggles at the amount of time, energy, imagination it took to build the place. I never cease wondering at New York.

Aristotle was right: we should approach the world first with wonder, only later with doubt. If you are in the throes of the blues, see if you haven't gotten the order reversed. If you are approaching the world first with doubt, your sense of wonder could well be atrophying. "The world does not lack for wonders, only for a sense of wonder." Søren Kierkegaard said much the same: "The greatest miracles in the world take place there where people say, 'I don't see anything so miraculous about that.'"

So for those of you trying to beat the blues, I have a very simple wish: between now and next Sunday, have a "wonder-full" week.

If wonder can do wonders against the blues, so too can anger. Of course, depression and boredom are both linked to anger, but to anger that is repressed. Repressed anger is lethal. A discerning friend of mine once remarked, "A thought-murder a day keeps the psychiatrist away." She was drawing the all-important line between feelings and behavior, insisting that while all behavior is not valid, all feelings are. Her words reminded me of St. Paul's, "Be angry, but do not sin" (Eph. 4:26). Actually, if we're never angry we probably are sinning; for just as the world does not lack for wonders, so it is hardly short of things to be mad about. Jesus never tolerated the intolerable and neither should we. Anger is not only a good counter to depression; given the madness and massive immoralities in which we are presently immersed, only a moral passion akin to Christ's can save our sanity.

Some years ago, an overly polite father, who had never been able to get close to his son, one day reported that he and his son had ended up rolling all over the floor in a fight. He was horrified, but I rather rejoiced. To be sure, that's not the best way for a father to get in touch with his son. But contact is contact; politeness can be a barrier more devastating than a blow.

Some people are afraid of being angry at their friends for fear of losing them. Well, isn't it better to be hated for what we are than loved for what we are not? And is not a true friend one who risks his friendship for the sake of his friend?

Henry Thoreau is remembered as a man who never trimmed the truth. Like Jesus, he never tolerated hypocrisy. Jesus said, "Woe to you, scribes and Pharisees, hypocrites" (Matt. 23:25). Thoreau said, "For every virtuous person, there are 999 patrons of virtue." Jesus said, "Not all who say 'Lord, Lord' shall enter the kingdom of heaven" (Matt. 7:21). Thoreau wrote of the New Testament: "Most people favor it outwardly, defend it with bigotry, and hardly ever read it."

Unheeded and unpopular in his time, Thoreau is today honored because he put something of substance into the mainstream of American history that sustains us over a hundred years later. Like Jesus he never repressed his anger, but he did keep it focused. Like Jesus too, he was willing to risk his friendships for the sake of his friends.

So, all of you trying to beat the blues: Have not only a wonder-full week; have a feisty one too. "Be angry, but do not sin."

Most of all, start loving someone. You know how it is, when psychologically you are on dead center, when you cannot move. In such moments it's important to do something, if only to clean a room. But when you're really depressed, you've got to try to do something for someone else. Visit someone in the hospital, write a fan letter to someone about whose good deed or words you read in the morning paper, take someone to the movies, contribute to some country's relief.

Of course it won't save the world, but that's not your business. Ultimately, we are not called upon to save the world. Ultimately, we are called on to do what's right, only penultimately to be effective. And how we get that order reversed! Imagine Socrates, as they handed him the hemlock, saying, "Hold everything, is Plato going to write me up?" Imagine Nathan Hale, stopping execution proceedings to inquire, "Are the thirteen colonies going to win? Is every kid in the new country going to memorize the last words I am now about to utter?"

I know how easy it is to get depressed, especially when the world appears ready to go down the drain and there seems to be so little any of us can do about it. Half the time when I stand up to plead for a disarmed planet, I feel like Rocinante, a tired hack of a horse being ridden by a quixotic idea. But then, who but God knows how effective any of us is going to be in anything we do? What we do know is that love is a necessity as well as a command; that love is like the loaves and fishes—there is never enough until we start sharing; and that of Jesus, our Lord and Savior, it is fair to say that "all the armies that ever marched, all the navies that ever sailed, all the kings that ever reigned and all the parliaments that ever sat have not so affected humanity as has that one solitary loving life."

That thought is enough to snap me right out of it, to make me want to say all over again, "Bless the Lord, all his works, in all places of his dominion. Bless the Lord, O my soul."

Dear Christians, go out and have a wonderful, feisty, and loving week. And may God bless you.

# 10. Wrestling with the Devil

Reading:   Luke 4:1–13

One of the livelier Christological debates in the history of the church revolves around the question, "Was Jesus ever really tempted?" The sides line up as follows: One group says, *No posse pecare*—Jesus was not able to sin; the other counters, *Posse non pecare*—he was able not to sin. It boils down to this: If Jesus' will was so attuned to God's that he was not able to sin, then obviously he was not really tempted. On the other hand, if he was perfectly capable of sin—but didn't—then he was really tempted; tempted, in fact, more than any of us, for who better measures the strength of temptation—he who eventually throws in the towel, or the one who contends to the very end?

Personally, I see little point to the debate. If Jesus wasn't really tempted, then he wasn't really human; for what else is at the core of human life if not the agony of choice? And if Jesus wasn't really tempted, then Luke's story is, as they say, "sheer hagiographical imagination," or worse yet, a fraud. For the story could have come to the disciples from nowhere else but from the lips of Jesus himself, no one else having witnessed his struggle.

So I suggest we accept the description of Jesus found in Hebrews "one, who in every respect has been tempted as we are, yet without sin" (Heb. 4:15). In other words, *posse non pecare!*

The next thing to say is that this story has little to do with temptations as we generally understand them. (Who was it who said, "Everything I like is immoral, indecent, or fattening?") This is big-time stuff. This is a large-scale attack that the Devil is mounting—and, fiendishly enough, at the point of Jesus' greatest vulnerability, his identity. Only a few days before, when he was baptized, Jesus received, as we all do in baptism, his identity. He heard, 'Thou art my beloved son" (Luke 3:22). Now he hears, "*If* you are the son of God." In other words, the Devil is testing not the worst, but the very best in Jesus, his faith and commitment. Can't you hear him casting doubt: "Come on, Jesus, how can you, a penniless, uneducated Galilean carpenter—how can you possibly be the long-awaited Messiah? Who is going to believe you?"

Had I been in Jesus' place, I know I would have been sorely tested, because I know how hard it is to hang on to your calling when all odds favor your failure.

But let me interrupt the narrative in order to introduce the Devil to the one or two of you who may think you have not met him or her. (If God is androgenous, so is the Devil!) By way of introduction, let me say four things very briefly. The Devil is pictured as a person because evil is experienced as an intensely personal power, in the same way that God is a person because God is experienced as personal power. Second, the Devil is given a separate existence not because evil exists outside of us, but because evil is both in us and experienced as something greater than us. Third, the Devil is pictured as a fallen angel, because evil does not arise in our so-called lower nature, but in our spiritual nature, always seeking to corrupt our freedom. And finally, the Devil is exceedingly subtle, rarely suggesting we do anything bad. On the contrary, the Devil invariably suggests we do something eminently reasonable. After all, Eve only took the apple when she saw that it was "good for food, pleasing to the eye, and much to be desired to make people wise" (Gen. 3:6).

So I am going to assume that the first of Christ's three temptations—to turn stones into bread—was neither to use his powers selfishly, nor, as is often suggested, to win followers by material gifts. Rather, I view it as a temptation to compromise one's calling by substituting the good in place of the best. Had I been Jesus, the Devil, I'm sure, would soon have had me reasoning as follows: "Why shouldn't I give my people bread? God knows how poor they are, as do I, having been born into their poverty. Didn't God help Moses with manna, and isn't the Messiah expected to do even more than Moses? Dear God, you have me running counter to all expectations. And how can I possibly say to a bunch of starving people, 'I am the bread of life, he who cometh to me shall never hunger?' That's unconscionable, God, and you know it."

As the above sounds so reasonable, so realistic, I'm sure I would have capitulated. But Jesus—*posse non pecare*—Jesus, who, again and again, was to feed the hungry, at that moment may have remembered that it was only after they were filled with manna that the Israelites rebelled. Only after their bellies were full did they doubt their high calling.

Here is a wise word from the Russian theologian, Nikolay Aleksandrovich Berdyayev, "When bread is assured, then God becomes a hard and inescapable reality, instead of an escape from harsh reality." When bread is assured, then the contrast between the good and the best becomes sharp. The contrast may be a little overdrawn here, but let's end the discussion of this first temptation with these words from playwright Herb Gardner. In his play *A Thousand Clowns*, the character who has made his no-questions-asked peace with the world for thirty thousand dollars a year, speaks to his ne'er-do-well brother, Murray, who has rebelled against the deceits of conventional society and cares passionately about people.

I have long been aware, Murray, I have long been aware that you don't respect me much. I suppose there are a lot of brothers who don't get along. Unfortunately for you, Murray, you want to be a hero. Maybe if a fellow falls into a lake, you can jump in and save him. There is still that kind of stuff. But who gets opportunities like that in mid-town Manhattan, with all that traffic? I am willing to deal with the available world and I do not choose to shake it up but to live with it. There are the people who spill things and the people who get spilled on. I choose not to notice the stains, Murray. I have a wife and two children, and business, like they say, is business. I am not an exceptional man, so it is possible for me to stay with things the way they are. I am lucky; I am gifted. I have a talent for surrender. I am at peace. But you are cursed, and, as I like you, it makes me sad. You don't have this gift. And I see the torture of it. All I can do is worry for you, but I will not worry for myself. You cannot convince me that I am one of the bad guys. I get up, I go, I lie a little, I peddle a little, I watch the rules, I talk the talk. We fellows have those offices high up there so that we can catch the wind and go with it, however it blows. But, and I will not apologize for it, I take pride. I am the best possible Arnold Burns.

The Devil is always urging us to be realistic, to be reasonable, to compromise the calling we received in baptism, to allow the good to usurp the place of the best.

The second temptation is like unto the first. The Devil takes Jesus up to a high place, shows him all the kingdoms of the world in a moment of time, and claims that they all belong to him—a very interesting assertion. Then he says, "Here, I'll make them yours." Once again, with a little imagination, we can see the Devil suggesting that something good and tangible is probably better than the best, which is wildly utopian anyhow. Had we lived as Jews under the rod of Rome, we surely would have longed for political liberation. Many of our fathers, uncles, grandfathers would have been numbered among the 100,000 people who perished in the abortive rebellions between the years 67 and 37 B.C. Like almost everybody else, we would have been expecting a political messiah, to implement the word and will of God as prophesied by Zechariah: "The Lord will set free all the families of Judah. . . . On that day, I, the Lord, will set about destroying all the nations that come against Jerusalem" (Zech. 12:19).

Why not? Putting myself in Jesus' place, I think I would have continued to reason that just as you can't talk to starving people about bread from heaven, so you cannot in good conscience talk about the Kingdom of God to people whose kingdom is under alien and harsh rule.

So I understand the temptation today, for instance, to listen to that devilish realism, which maintains that Americans must increase their military might lest they fall under alien rule. "It's too bad, but after all the Russians don't understand nonviolence." Still, I am troubled, because we Christians receive our identity from the Son of God who refused worldly power based on violence. Therefore the question is real: Should American Christians pay taxes to support the Pentagon's rising budget? Or should they rather heed their own prophet Martin Luther King, Jr., who warned:

through violence, you may murder the liar but you cannot murder the lie, nor establish the truth. Through violence, you may murder the hater, but you do not murder hate. Returning violence for violence, multiplies violence, adding deeper darkness to a night already devoid of stars. Darkness cannot drive out darkness, only light can do that. Hate cannot drive out hate, only love can do that. (From *Where Do We Go from Here?*)

Again we must ask ourselves if the Devil has not persuaded us that the good should usurp the best because it is more realistic. At the outset of World War II, I stood with the poet Charles Peguy: "People who insist on keeping their hands clean are likely to find themselves without hands." And forty years later, I am still fearful of putting purity above relevance. But much has passed in forty years, and in the nuclear age it may be that nothing short of the best is relevant. As God is not mocked, we shouldn't be surprised that the day is dawning when the so-called ethics of perfection are becoming ethics of survival. When we live at each other's mercy, we had better learn to be merciful. If we don't learn to be meek, who is going to inherit the earth?

Finally, in the third temptation, we see the Devil suggesting that Christ's goodness be made clear to all beyond the shadow of a doubt. If the Son of God is not to rescue people from their poverty, nor to liberate them from their tyranny, if the Messiah is to disappoint so many messianic expectations, then at least let him be vindicated. Let God prove that this is what goodness is all about. At the very least, let God shield his beloved from harm. It's only fair.

Indeed it is. But to insist on fairness is like insisting on justice for the hungry, and on freedom for the oppressed. It's right, it's good, but it's not good enough. Fortunately for us (because we're not exactly fair with God), God goes far beyond fairness in his dealings with us. Fortunately for us, God's love exceeds what's demanded by justice, his forgiveness never fails. Therefore he whose calling as the Son of God is to lay bare his father's heart for all to see, must needs take up his cross, and be "despised and rejected of men" (Isa. 53:3). God does prove himself, but in the power of his love.

It's hard, isn't it? It is very hard to be a Christian. "Whither, relentless, wilt thou still be driving thy maimed and halt that have not strength to go?" It's very hard to be a Christian, but on the other hand it's too dull to be anything less. It's very hard to bear the agony of choice, but it's inhuman to refuse it. So, in this tough time of testing in the Christian year, let's see if we can't find a little more courage to stand against the insidious realism of the Devil, to resist what at first blush always appears so reasonable, to refuse to allow the good to usurp the place of the best. And of one thing we may be sure: As to Jesus so to us, angels will come ministering when the struggle is over.

# 11.  We Know Not What We Do

Readings:   Psalm 130
            Luke 5:1–8

Had you to summarize the events of Palm Sunday, Maundy
Thursday, Good Friday, and Easter, you'd be hard-pressed to
find a phrase more apt than the one Paul used writing to
Christians in Rome: "Where sin increased, grace abounded all
the more" (Romans 5:20). When religious leaders plot to destroy the Son of God and the State washes its hands, when
one disciple betrays and all others desert, when the crowd
makes March weather look like a model of reliability—then sin
increases, and the cross becomes the foremost sign of sin,
proving our inhumanity to one another is exceeded only by
our inhumanity to God. Yet the foremost sign of sin is also
the chief symbol of God's grace. For the cross tells us that you
can kill God's love but you cannot keep it dead and buried;
that there are more important tragedies than the tragedy of
death and no victory more important than the triumph of love.
The cross tells us that where sin increases, grace abounds all
the more.

I want to speak of Christ's first "word" from the cross, the
one that speaks most directly to this triumph of love. You
remember that even as the nails are being driven into his
hands, Jesus prays, "Father, forgive them, for they know not
what they do" (Luke 23:34). I'm always stunned by people's
ability to get all flustered about the Immaculate Conception,
the Virgin Birth, the physical resurrection of Jesus, his chang-
ing the water into wine, and yet, without batting an eye, they
can stand up and say, "I believe in the forgiveness of sins"—
as if there were nothing to it!

Let's start by asking, "Who is 'they' in 'Father, forgive them for they know what they do'?" Unlike too many city-dwellers today, Jesus didn't die at the hands of muggers or rapists, leaders of organized crime, or other thugs: he fell into the well-scrubbed hands of ministers and lawyers, statesmen and professors—society's most respected members. So when we ask ourselves, "Were you there when they crucified my Lord?" the answer has to be, "You bet I was, hammer in hand." "They" is us, and we know not what we do—probably the most devastating comment ever made on the stupidity of self-respecting folk. And we know not what we do, because we know not who we are!

It's not that our information is poor, only that our hearts are hard, our wills are weak, and our imagination is almost non-existent. In a memorable passage in *Wind, Sand and Stars*, the French poet-aviator Antoine de St.-Exupery, muses to himself as he rides in a bus with government officials and clerks:

Old bureaucrat, my comrade, it is not you who are to blame. No one ever helped you to escape. You, like the termite, built your peace by blocking up with cement every chink and cranny through which the light might pierce. You rolled yourself up into a ball in your genteel security, in routine, in the stifling conventions of provincial life raising a modest rampart against the wind and the tides and the stars. You have chosen not to be perturbed by great problems, having trouble enough to forget your own fate as man. You are not the dweller upon an errant planet and do not ask yourself questions to which there are no answers. You are a petty bourgeois of Toulouse. Nobody grasped you by the shoulder while there was still time. Now the clay of which you were shaped has dried and hardened, and naught in you will ever awaken the sleeping musician, the poet, the astronomer that possibly inhabited you in the beginning.

Do you see your life reflected? It's as if we settled for this horrible March weather, forgetting the outburst of riotous beauty that lies just ahead. It's as if, listening to Liberace, we thought we were hearing Horowitz. It's as if, in reading the chirping optimism of the *Reader's Digest*, we thought we were approaching the heights of Dante's *Divine Comedy*. No wonder we crucify Christ. We crucify Jesus, the best among us, only because first we crucify the best within us, and then don't want to be reminded. We make a great mistake every time we think death the great tragedy. It's the "little deaths," the good things that die while we yet live, that are so tragic. I said that there were no victories more important than the triumph of love. But we defeat all chances for this triumph fearing failure more than we love life. We deny our faith by not daring to live beyond self-concern. And then when someone like Jesus does shake us by the shoulder, forcing us to face the bitter fruits of caution, the vacant years, the ugly altars to ourselves, our nation's lunatic lust for place and possessions, we crucify him in the time-honored tradition of ancient kings who killed the bearer of bad news.

Either that, or we come to our senses, repent, and plead with the psalmist, "Lord hear my voice. Let thine ear be attentive to the voice of my supplication" (Ps. 130:2). I love the way Simon Peter, when he saw in the miraculous catch of fish the beauty and power of Jesus, fell to his knees and cried, 'Go, Lord, leave me, sinner that I am" (Luke 5:8). For a kneeling person is one who realizes how truly tall human beings can stand. A kneeling person is a victor over his pride, a seeker looking above herself to find herself. A kneeling person is the only person who can honestly say, "I believe in the forgiveness of sin."

Dear Christians, let us not hesitate to kneel as frequently as necessary in this Lenten season, in order to find out what we have become, and who we might yet be. We need to kneel because we are tied in knots by a chain of past mistakes, because we are dominated by what we have been rather than by thoughts of what we might become. We need to kneel to receive fresh chances and the grace to make good those chances. We need to kneel because if we don't save our souls we'll never save the world.

The world can only be saved by those who know that there

are more important tragedies than the tragedy of death, and no victories more important than the triumph of love. The world will be saved, if Christians become as Christ can make them. The world will be saved if, by the grace of God, Christians do not refuse their own crosses, but allow them to become lightening rods to ground the world's hate—because they are determined, as was Christ himself, that where sin increases grace will all the more abound. The world will be saved by those who, knowing who they are, can say, Christlike, from a cross, "Father, forgive them, for they know not what they do."

O God, may we go to our knees out of a deep sense of no other place to go. And when we fall on our knees with our face to the rising sun, O Lord, have mercy on us, lift us up again, and keep us on the paths of righteousness, even if they lead to Jerusalem and to a cross. Amen.

# 12. The Grace of Dependency

Reading:   Luke 23:32–43

"Jesus, remember me . . . 'Truly, I say to you, today you will be with me in Paradise' " (Luke 23:42–43).

And here's a commentary from St. Augustine which surely warms the heart and also chills the blood: "Two criminals were crucified with Christ. One was saved; do not despair. One was not; do not presume."

About these two criminals we know absolutely nothing, a fact that hasn't prevented pious speculation from building whole biographies about the one whose eleventh-hour discovery of Christ allows us to say of him, in words of Shakespeare, "Nothing in his life became him like the leaving of it." But I'm not of a mind to slight the other criminal. Perhaps he was an associate of Barabbas, the revolutionary hero released that same morning at the behest of the crowd. Perhaps he was a high-minded freedom fighter, determined to see Israel's independence, or Rome leveled by his attempts to gain it. In any case, he shows a defiant spirit of the kind Dylan Thomas wanted his father to show even as his own life expired:

> Do not go gentle into that good night,
> Rage, rage against the dying of the light.

This criminal raged all right, no whiner, he was a fighter to the end.

But having said that, we have to go on to recognize that defiance is only a step on the way to freedom, not freedom itself. We have also to recognize, once again, that our human best tends to be at odds with what we might call the holy best. In a sensitive spiritual autobiography, *The Sacred Journey*, Frederick Buechner writes:

> . . . to do for yourself the best that you have in you to do—to grit your teeth and clench your fists in order to survive the world at its harshest and worst—is, by that very act, to be unable to let something be done for you and in you that is more wonderful still. The trouble with steeling yourself against the harshness of reality is that the same steel that secures your life against being destroyed secures your life also against being opened up and transformed by the holy power that life itself comes from. You can survive on your own. You can grow stronger on your own. You can even prevail on your own. But you cannot become human on your own.

In other words, to become human you have to go beyond self-sufficiency to know the grace of dependency. The defiant criminal couldn't be saved because a clenched fist cannot accept a helping hand.

Many of us can identify with this criminal, as many of us tend to be a bit too self-sufficient, too defiant. But today let us see if we can identify with the one who asked for a helping hand. Let's start by recalling another criminal, the most renowned perhaps in all of Western literature—Raskolnikov, the hero of Dostoyevski's *Crime and Punishment*. As textbooks are quick to point out, *raskolnik* in Russian means a split personality. What few add is that a *raskolnik* is also a heretic. In Russian *raskol* means heresy, and heresy is derived from the Greek verb meaning "to sieze," as for example a town. Dostoyevski certainly knew what he was doing when he gave his hero a name with a double meaning, a name not found in any Moscow telephone directory.

What is heresy? Contrary to what many people believe, Dostoyevski did not consider it an intellectual matter, but rather a psychological one. What mattered to him was less the position taken, than the motives for taking it. (You seize a town, generally, for yourself and at somebody else's expense). Likewise, to Dostoyevski, crime was only a superficial breaking of the law. More profoundly, as he saw it, to commit a crime was to rend the bond of love. Therefore the punishment for crime was less the isolation imposed by barred windows than the isolation imposed by the thick walls of a heart grown hard. The punishment for rending the bond of love is to experience the bond of love rent. It doesn't matter what form the egotism takes: It can be self-exaltation, as with Raskolnikov, or self-abasement. (I'm sure Dostoyevski would have loved what a modern Russian, Eugenia Ginzburg, wrote: "The egotism of those who suffer is probably even more all-embracing than the self-regard of those who are happy.") In all its forms, egotism has one punishment—isolation, the isolation of those who have cut themselves off from God, from their neighbors, and from their own loving selves, that part in each of us that delights in making a gift of itself. Hence egotists are heretics, and heretics have split personalities. They are *raskolniki*.

Now let us return to the scene on Calvary. The criminal is on his cross because he has rent the bond of love. Jesus is on his because he can only love. The criminal is on a cross of isolation, Jesus on one of vulnerability. The criminal is experiencing the agony of sin, Christ the cost of devotion. Then he who is guilty hears the victim of injustice (the greatest the world has known) pray for the forgiveness of his executioners. "Father, forgive them for they know not what they do." Such unconditional love proves too much for his hardened heart, which breaks. Instead of seeking to prevail, as did his fellow criminal, he becomes human. He cries out, "Jesus, remember me." And Jesus does, performing in his last hour, on a cross, his last healing miracle; "Today you will be with me in Paradise."

In portraying the myth of creation on the ceiling of the Sistine chapel, Michelangelo pictures the bond of love as it was first established—so easily, so naturally. Surrounded by cherubim and seraphim, God simply reaches down his hand from heaven to touch Adam's own upward-turned hand. But the bond, once rent, is not so easily restored. Sin has its price, and so has forgiveness. Reconciliation takes place on two crosses when a human being in agony stretches out his or her hand to Christ and says, "Jesus, remember me," and Christ from his cross stretches out his hand and says, "Today, you shall be with me in Paradise." That's what atonement—at-one-ment—is all about.

And of course those same words could have been exchanged had Christ and the criminal both had fifty more years to live. For Paradise is less a future promise than it is a present possibility. Paradise is the presence of God; hell, God's absence. Heaven and hell—both begin here—now.

All this strikes me as terribly important to us Americans here and how. I say "Americans" because while all of us have sins and sorrows, they are universal, and I have in mind some particular national sins and sorrows. Many of us Americans feel that ours is a large country, but one presently ruled by small minds, and for too long by leaders too eager for power to be trusted with it. Abroad, our solutions have exceeded the problems. We have sounded global alarms over local fires, while at home the reverse is true: We think to solve the problems of the poor with the crumbs that fall from the tables of the rich. As the poet Livy said of ancient Rome, our country can bear neither its ills nor the remedies that might cure them. As a result, the personal lives of many of us have taken a turn for the worse: We're nervous, tense, angry, we're getting poorer, closer to unemployment, to divorce—you fill in the particulars.

The temptation in bad times is to steel ourselves against the harshness of reality. But listen again to Buechner: "The trouble with steeling yourself against the harshness of reality is that the same steel that secures your life against being destroyed secures your life also against being opened up and transformed by the holy power that life itself comes from. You can survive on your own. You can grow stronger on your own. You can even prevail on your own. But you cannot become human on your own."

In inhumane times, we must stay human. Rather than become defiantly self-sufficient, we must learn the grace of dependency. Once again, a clenched fist cannot accept a helping hand. So let me ask you: Are you on a cross of pain, of sin, of sorrow, whether of society's making or your own? Then stretch out your hand to Jesus on his cross right next to yours. Say, "Jesus, remember me. I want to stay vulnerable, tender, loving, human." And he will reply, "Today, you shall be with me in Paradise. I'll drain your heart of fear and bitterness, filling it instead with that joy that can absorb all sorrow, with my peace that the world can neither give nor take away. For lo, I am with you always—cross by cross—unto the end of the age."

This atonement, this at-one-ment, is a daily possibility. "Jesus, remember me." "Today, you shall be with me in Paradise." Just think: instead of being in Hell, we can live in Heaven, even while we are still on earth! Praise be to God!

> Thy mercy, Lord, is great and far
> above the heavens. Let none be
> made ashamed that wait upon thee. Amen.

# 13. Heroes and Heroines for God

Reading: John 12:19

As any writer will tell you, the essence of good writing is drama, and the essence of drama is conflict. And that's what makes the Palm Sunday story so dramatic. In the whole of Scripture, Calvary not excepted, there is no scene in which the people taking part have more conflicting ideas about what is going on. The Pharisees think they have a heretic on their hands, and a peculiarly obnoxious one; for Jesus is saying, in effect, that the real troublemakers in this world are not the ignorant and cruel, but the intelligent and corrupt, people like the Pharisees themselves. Quite naturally, they resist him, and will do so all the more vigorously after he "cleanses" the temple by chasing away the money changers, symbols of that oldest form of corruption—religion become subservient to profit-making. Yet for all their power, they are today powerless: "The Pharisees then said to one another, 'You see that you can do nothing; look, the whole world has gone after him' " (John 12:19).

Indeed, in the form of the Jerusalem multitudes, the world did go after him that day. That's why Palm Sunday is so festive an occasion. Yet were they cheering a religious leader, these multitudes? Were they praising a man who had searched their consciences, convinced their minds, and won over their hearts? Or were they following a political leader whose power had been proved by the story circulating through the streets of the city that he had actually raised a man named Lazarus from the dead? To be sure, they were carrying palms, symbols of peace; but then, the Roman authorities forbade the carrying of spears. To be sure, they were praising God; but they were also hailing the King of Israel. Some of them no doubt remembered the prophesy of Zechariah: "Behold, your king is coming to you, humble, and riding on an ass" (Zech. 9:9). But I'll bet the majority had Saul and Solomon in mind. I'll bet the majority were hailing a new national leader come to help throw off the hated Roman yoke. And you can't blame any of them for wanting political independence. On the other hand, you can't equate such a political leader with "the Lamb of God that taketh away the sins of the world" (John 1:29).

With these differing perceptions went differing emotions. The Pharisees were sullen, the multitudes ecstatic. But the greatest contrast is between the crowds and Jesus. While they shout wildly, "Hosannah, blessed is he who comes in the name of the Lord, even the King of Israel," the King—instead of smiling and acknowledging the cheers—the King weeps.

And when he drew near and saw the city he wept over it, saying, "Would that even today you knew the things that make for peace! But now they are hid from your eyes. For the days shall come upon you, when your enemies will cast up a bank about you and surround you, and hem you in on every side, and dash you to the ground, you and all your children within you, and they will not leave one stone upon another in you; because you did not know the time of your visitation" (Luke 19:41–44).

Had Jesus wept only for what he had earlier predicted would befall him, that would be poignant enough. Instead, he weeps for what he is sure will befall the very people who today are urging him on; and who tomorrow, because of their blindness, will be shouting, "Crucify him!"

I suppose all this confusion shouldn't surprise us. Each of us is a walking civil war. We are so confused that Pascal could say of the world that it divides itself between saints who know they are sinners and sinners who imagine themselves to be saints. The Passion story teaches us the deepest lesson about ourselves and our political life. It is not that good is "forever on the scaffold, wrong upon the throne"; it is that all people stand in need of a merciful God, and that all politics should begin with repentance and forgiveness.

Fundamentally, we all need to confess that we are creatures trying to deny our creatureliness. Each of us is trying to overcome a sense—and a false sense, at that—of insignificance. Do you remember the day the first space shuttle got off the ground? It was a stirring sight, and stunning to realize that our earthbound days were coming to an end. But then came President Reagan's message to the space-bound astronauts: "You go in the hand of God." That was modest enough, but he went on: "Through you today we all feel as giants once again." Catch the sense of insignificance? "Once again we feel the surge of pride that comes from knowing we are the first and we are the best and we are so because we are free."

Not only Americans, but every people wants to feel they are the first and the best and free; and every space shuttle and every missile, every bomb and every human edifice—be it constructed of brick or of ideas—all are attempts, in part, to defy our underlying sense of helplessness, the terror we all feel before inevitable death. So in order to feel significant we have to scapegoat others into insignificance—into being second and not so free—because that surging pride of which the president spoke is not accidentally but essentially competitive. "Everybody has his Jew," said Arthur Miller in *Incident at Vichy*; "even the Jews have their Jews," someone to degrade, to humiliate, in order to raise us above the status of creature. All humanly caused evil is due to our attempts to deny our creatureliness. It is based on heroics. We want to make the world what it can never be: a place free from accident, a place free from impurity, a place free from death.

So is the answer to avoid all heroics? No, the answer is to be a hero or a heroine for God—for the sake of no one less than God, and in such a fashion that only the eyes of God need see. Anyone who needs more than God as a witness is too ambitious! And isn't the perfect illustration of that kind of heroism the story of Jesus riding into Jerusalem on Palm Sunday? He could have stayed in Galilee where it was safer; but he chose instead to take his words and deeds into the capital, into the very heart of entrenched religious and political power. He could have come on a horse, as a wartime king; but he chose instead to come in peace, for peace. He could have saved Israel; but he chose instead to save the world. He could have come with violence; but rather than inflict suffering, he chose to take suffering upon himself. What can only be said cynically of another—"It is better that one man should die than an entire nation perish"—can be said in utter truthfulness about oneself: "It is better that I should die rather than a single other person."

There is nothing wrong in being heroes and heroines for God. The danger lies in denying God through a combination of great moral vigor with little self-knowledge. Reinhold Niebuhr wrote: "Ultimately considered, evil is done not so much by evil people, but by good people who do not know themselves." But if we start on our knees we can rise to great heights; we can "rise and shine and give God the glory." Read it and you will find that the Gospel of John is full of heroic language, and Christ himself speaks tender but heroic words, proving thereby that only the truly strong can be tender. "In the world you have tribulation, but be of good cheer, I have overcome the world" (John 16:33).

Listen also to these words spoken in Jerusalem just before his death: "Father, the hour has come; glorify thy son that the Son may glorify Thee, since thou hast given him power over all flesh, to give eternal life to all whom thou hast given him. And this is eternal life, that they know Thee the only true God, and Jesus Christ whom thou hast sent" (John 17:1).

There it is—the whole goal of life: to know God as the only true God, and to know him through Jesus Christ, the King of Kings and Lord of Lords, riding into Jerusalem on the back of a donkey.

On that Palm Sunday and on the days that follow in Jerusalem, in Jesus' words and deeds we see transparently the power of God at work—empowering the weak, scorning the powerful, healing the hurt, taking upon himself the sin and suffering of the world. And just as Christ's knowledge still lights our path, and his faith lives on in our hearts, so his tasks have now fallen to our hands. Our hands are important. Without us the glorious space shuttle will surely turn into another inglorious weapons system. Without us, humanity will come to judgment not before God but before the atom. Without us, the poor will continue to get poorer, the rich richer. New York will never become that "golden city with milk and honey blest." But with reason, with restraint and faith that God can endow our lives with significance, we may yet see the world around, "alabaster cities gleam undimmed by human tears." We may hear again the words of the Pharisees: "Look, the world has gone after him" (John 12:19).

Can we still celebrate Palm Sunday, knowing how confused the scene was, and how the story ends? Yes, because with a better understanding of what was going on, we have even more to cheer about. The cross of Christ says something terrible about us, but something wonderful about God. It symbolizes not only the triumph in defeat of a good man. It also represents the merciful action of a loving Father: "For God was in Christ, reconciling the world unto himself" (2 Cor. 5:19). Therefore, with joy shining through tears, we can sing,

> Ride on, ride on in majesty;
> Thy last and fiercest strife is nigh;
> Bow thy meek head to mortal pain,
> Then take, O Christ, thy power and reign.*

---

* From Henry H. Milman's hymn "Ride On, Ride On in Majesty."

# 14. "I Thirst"

Of the last seven words of Christ spoken from the cross, only the fifth could have been said by any one of us. In the Gospel of John (John 19:28) we read: "After this, Jesus, knowing that all was now finished, said 'I thirst.' "

Not even Martin Luther King, Jr., whose death we recall with renewed sorrow at this time of year—not even King would have cried out, "My God, my God, why has thou forsaken me?" For in the eyes of all but a few, this Nobel Prize winner died a just man, a prophet of God. It was the heathen, not the believers who rejected Martin. But Christ was rejected by the religious, at least by their leaders, who rejected him in the name of God as godless, in the name of Holy Law as a law-breaker. Religious rejection—that's real rejection of the kind that must have created the doubt that prompted the cry "My God, my God, why . . . ?"

In contrast, all of us could have said, "I thirst." The words reflect sheer physical need. They have nothing to do with God, with love and faith. Yet on the lips of the crucified Son of God, don't they have everything to do with God, with love and faith?

When you think of God, what image comes to mind? Is it the grandfather figure of your childhood? Michelangelo's powerful heavenly figure? Maybe when you think of God no image at all comes to mind. One thing only is clear: When we think of God, we don't generally think of a bleeding, dying figure asking for someone to moisten his burning lips.

Several years ago a man named J. B. Phillips wrote a book called *Your God is Too Small*. It was a good book, and made the often forgotten point that God is not a god of the few, nor of the many, but the God of all of us, the God who also laid the foundations of the earth and scattered stars in the heavens greater in number than all the inhabitants of the world, the God of whom we sing, "Heaven and earth are full of thy glory; glory be to Thee, O Lord most high."

But today, Good Friday, is the time to say, "Your God is too big." Your God is too big to keep his eye on the sparrow, too big to care about every abused child, too big to worry about the children the world around—and there are millions of them—who never so much as open their mouths to say "aah" to a doctor. On Good Friday, we should recognize that the perfect image of the mighty, transcendent, invisible God is "I thirst" on the lips of the Son of God. For those two words from the cross lay bare the heart of God for all to see. They show us that God shares the lot of the least of us—the handicapped children, the old on welfare, the hungry, the dying. God suffers with us. More than that, God suffers for us. "I thirst" on the lips of Christ is the perfect image of a loving God, for as St. Paul says, "in him (Christ) all the fulness of God was pleased to dwell, and through him to reconcile to himself all things, whether on earth or in heaven, making peace by the blood of his cross" (Col. 1:19–20).

Why do we normally reject such an image, accepting instead images of God that are sentimental or powerful, that do not accord with a truly loving God? Is it because we want to be immune from such suffering ourselves? Maybe we want to think of God as powerful, feeling as we often do that only power impresses, only success succeeds. But by idolizing power we dehumanize ourselves, thereby making it necessary for God to come to earth in human form to take our inhumanity upon himself, in order to make us human again. Maybe we simply want to keep God up there in the heavens where we can praise him, far away from earth where we might have to follow him.

Whatever our reasons, they are belied by Good Friday, which reminds us that we are not going to be helped by God's power, only by God's weakness. For power can only *force* us to do things. Only love can *move* us to do things. Power affects behavior, love the heart. And nothing on earth so moves the heart as suffering love. That is why the perfect expression of God's love for us is the dying figure of God's love incarnate pleading for someone to moisten his burning lips.

And someone does. Someone runs to soak a sponge in sour wine and holds it up, on the end of a cane, to Jesus' lips. In the Gospel of John the act is recorded as a gracious one, perhaps the only act of human mercy in the whole Passion story. And it has, I believe, a special significance. Whenever we celebrate the Lord's Supper, we receive the cup of Christ. Christ puts wine on our lips. But whoever puts wine on the lips of Christ understands the mutuality of communion. We need our Savior, who also needs us. For there are thirsty figures on crosses all around this globe, and "inasmuch as ye have done it unto the least of these my brothers and sisters ye have done it unto me" (Matt. 25:40).

Obviously, we should dedicate ourselves to the task of cutting down these crosses of racism, classism, ageism, sexism, nationalism, on which millions of our fellow human beings are daily being crucified. But for today it is enough to stand at the foot of our Savior's cross. "Were you there when they crucified my Lord?" I have suggested that we all were, hammer in hand. But now let us lay down our hammers, and take up the sponge and put wine on the lips of our suffering Savior, recognizing in him the perfect expression of the God who pours out his heart for every last one of us. "For in him all the fulness of God was pleased to dwell, and through him to reconcile to himself all things, whether on earth or in heaven, making peace by the blood of his cross."

# 15. Like Him We Rise

Readings:  Matthew 28
1 Corinthians 15:17–18, 20

In Haydn's oratorio *The Seasons*, in the section called "Spring," the chorus sings, "As yet the year is unconfirmed, and oft-returning winter's blast the bud and bloom destroy"—an apt description of this blustering day. But no matter: we know that energy soon will be pouring out of the ground and into every blade of grass, into every flower, bush, and tree; we know that soon the robins will join the pigeons, the sky will be full of the thunder of the sun, "the shaggy mountains will stomp their feet, the waves toss high and clap their wild blue hands." Overhead and underfoot and all around we shall soon see, hear, feel, and smell the juice and joy of spring.

But suppose this horrible weather were here to stay. Suppose that April had never come, that the earth somehow had spun out of orbit and was headed for the immensities of space, there forever to be assailed by winter's blasts. Not only would that be a gruesome prospect, but also, according to St. Paul, a proper analogy for the state of human affairs without Easter. Not one to hedge his bets, St. Paul puts all his Christian eggs in one Easter basket: "If Christ has not been raised, your faith is futile" (1 Cor. 15:17). Just as we know that April is coming, despite all appearances, because April is already here, so we know that we no longer live in a Good Friday world because Easter is already here.

God knows it continues to look like a Good Friday world. What makes the Good Friday story so devastating is that it is still so shockingly true. In totalitarian countries politicians have but to hear, "Thou art not Caesar's friend" (John 19:12, KJV), and away they fall like autumn leaves; while in more democratic countries, politicians seek to minimize their responsibilities, washing their hands and thereby plaiting the crown of thorns. Like Peter, most of us disciples follow our Lord halfway, but not the other half. As for the majority of citizens, are they not like the crowd that gathered on Calvary, not to cheer a miscarriage of justice, but also not to protest it? Failing to realize that compassion without confrontation is hopelessly sentimental, the people go home beating their breasts, preferring guilt to responsibility.

By all appearances, it is a Good Friday world. But by the light of Easter, through the thick darkness covering the nations, we can dimly discern a "Yes, but" kind of message. Yes, fear and self-righteousness, indifference and sentimentality kill; but love never dies, not with God, and not even with us. The Easter message says that all the tenderness and strength which on Good Friday we saw scourged, buffeted, stretched out on a cross—all that beauty and goodness is again alive and with us now, not as a memory that inevitably fades, but as an undying presence in the life of every single one of us, if only we would recognize it. Christ's resurrection promises our own resurrection, for Christ is risen *pro nobis*, for us, to put love in our hearts, decent thoughts in our heads, and a little more iron up our spines. Christ is risen to convert us, not from life to something more than life, but from something less than life to the possibility of full life itself. As it is written: The glory of God is a human being fully alive.

We'll come to the actual Easter event, the empty tomb, but first it's necessary to emphasize that Easter has less to do with one person's escape from the grave than with the victory of seemingly powerless love over loveless power. And let us also emphasize this: Too often Easter comes across very sentimentally, like a dessert wafer—airy and sweet. But there's nothing sentimental about Easter. Easter represents a demand as well as a promise, a demand not that we sympathize with the crucified Christ, but that we pledge our loyalty to the risen one. That means an end to all loyalties, to all people, and all institutions that crucify. I don't see how you can proclaim allegiance to the Risen Lord and then allow life once again to lull you to sleep, to smother you in convention, to choke you with success. It seems to me that the burden of proof is with those who think they can combine loyalty to the Risen Christ with continuing the arms race; or with those who think that we Americans have the right to decide who lives, dies, and rules in other countries; or with those who think that the Risen Lord would not argue with an economic system that clearly reverses the priorities of Mary's Magnificat—filling the rich with good things and sending the poor empty away.

True loyalty to the Risen Lord is surely that displayed by Peter, who finally went the second half, who became ten times the person he was before Jesus' death; the loyalty of St. Stephen, who wasn't afraid of confrontation, and who under the rain of death-dealing stones cried out, Christlike, "Father, forgive"; the loyalty of so many early Christian men and women who, like Peter and Stephen, watered with their blood the seed of the church until it became the acorn that broke the mighty boulder that was the Roman Empire.

There is an Easter sunrise service that takes place on the edge of the Grand Canyon. As the Scripture line is read, "And an angel of the Lord descended from heaven and rolled back the stone" (Matt. 28:2), a giant boulder is heaved over the rim. As it goes crashing down the side of the Grand Canyon into the Colorado River far below, a two-thousand-voice choir bursts into the Hallelujah chorus. Too dramatic? Not if, despite all appearances, we live in an Easter world.

But let's move on with St. Paul's understanding of Easter. "If Christ has not been raised, your faith is futile, and you are still in your sins." I don't know why sin is such a bad word these days. Obviously, we're all sinners, the more so the more we try to deny it. But that's not the issue. At issue is whether there is more mercy in God than sin in us. And according to

Paul, just as love is stronger than death, so forgiveness is stronger than sin. That may be the hardest thing in the faith to believe. The empty tomb is as nothing compared to the fact that we are indeed forgiven. But think again of Peter. Peter denied Christ just as surely as Judas betrayed him. The difference is that Peter came back to receive his forgiveness. The tragedy of Judas is that he never did.

Easter proclaims that forgiveness is offered all of us exactly as it was Peter. Just think: All the rulers of the world are forgiven, and church people too—including the pastors and priests who frequently have God in their mouths, but not so frequently in their hearts. *All* are forgiven. What does that mean? It means that we are relieved not of the consequences of our sin, but of the consequences of being sinners. It means we are no longer sinners, but forgiven sinners. It means that with the zeal of gratitude we too can become ten times the people we are. It means that instead of trying to prove ourselves endlessly, we can express ourselves as fearless, vulnerable, dedicated, joyous followers of our risen Lord.

And now perhaps we can deal with the empty tomb. St. Paul was the earliest New Testament writer, and it is clear that his Resurrection faith, like the faith of the disciples, was not based on the negative argument of an empty tomb, but on the positive conviction that the Lord had appeared to him. It is also clear that Christ's appearances were not those of a resurrected corpse, but more akin to intense visionary experiences.

Not only Peter, but all the apostles after Jesus' death were ten times the people they were before; that's irrefutable. It was in response to their enthusiasm (the word means "in God") that the opposition organized; and it was in response to the opposition—so many scholars believe—that the doctrine of the empty tomb arose, not as a cause but as a consequence of the Easter faith. The last chapter of Matthew may be literally true—I don't want to dispute it—but I also don't want any of you to stumble forever over it. Like many a miracle story in the Bible, it may be an expression of faith rather than a basis of faith.

Convinced by his appearances that Jesus was their living Lord, the disciples really had only one category in which to articulate this conviction, and that was the doctrine of the resurrection of the dead. To St. Paul, the events of the last days had been anticipated and God, by a mighty act, had raised Jesus from the dead—in a spiritual body. In Paul's writings, the living Christ and the Holy Spirit are never clearly differentiated, so that when he says "Not I, but Christ who dwells within me," he is talking about the same Holy Spirit that you and I can experience in our own lives. I myself believe passionately in the resurrection of Jesus Christ, because in my own life I have experienced Christ not as a memory, but as a presence. So today on Easter we gather not, as it were, to close the show with the tune "Thanks for the memory," but rather to reopen the show, because "Jesus Christ is risen today."

There remains only to say a word about the final consequence Paul draws from the Resurrection. "If you are still in your sins, then those also who have fallen asleep . . . have perished" (1 Cor. 15:18). What then are we to say of those who have died, and how are we to anticipate our own death?

The Bible is at pains to point out that life ends: "All mortal flesh is as the grass" (Prov. 40:6). But St. Paul insists that "neither death nor life . . . can separate us from the love of God" (Rom. 8:38–39), that "whether we live or whether we die, we are the Lord's" (Rom. 14:8). If death, then, is no threat to our relationship to God, if, in the words of the Easter hymn, "made like him like him we rise, ours the cross, the grave, the skies"—then death should be no threat at all. If we don't know what is beyond the grave we do know *who* is beyond the grave, and Christ resurrected links the two worlds, telling us we really live only in one. If God's love is immortal, then life is eternal, and death is a horizon, and a horizon is nothing save the limit of our sight. Can we not then also proclaim with St. Paul's wonderful freedom,

Now this I say, sisters and brothers, that flesh and blood cannot inherit the Kingdom of God; neither doth corruption inherit incorruption. For this corruptible must put on incorruption, and this mortal must put on immortality. So when this corruptible shall have put on incorruption, and this mortal shall have put on immortality, then shall be brought to pass the saying that is written, Death is swallowed up in victory. O death, where is thy sting? O grave, where is thy victory? Thanks be to God who giveth us the victory through our Lord Jesus Christ (1 Cor. 15:50–57).

So sisters and brothers, what are we going to do on this blustery, glorious Easter Day? God has done God's part: Resurrection has overcome crucifixion, forgiveness sin; our departed loved ones are at rest where we too shall be some day. Are we going to continue the illusion of a Good Friday world, or start living the reality of an Easter one?

# 16. Mary and Jesus

Reading:   Luke 2:41–52

Just as "I'm Dreaming of a White Christmas" aspires to the status of a Christmas carol—that is, to be considered on a par with "Lo, How a Rose," and "Joy to the World"—so Mother's Day clamors for religious recognition, to be hailed as an official day on the church calendar. A brave preacher might try to buck the tide, turning perhaps to Philip Wylie: "Megaloid mom-worship has gotten completely out of hand." A brave preacher might even have fun reminding his or her congregation that "I want a girl just like the girl that married dear old Dad" is but one of the more naïve expressions of the Oedipus complex. But a smart preacher will go with the flow, turning to the old Jewish proverb: "God could not be everywhere, and therefore he made mothers." On this Mother's Day I have chosen to be smart.

The relationship between Jesus and Mary is hardly your everyday mother-son relationship. But it strikes me that three episodes in their life together speak to Mother's Day. The first is the story of Joseph and Mary returning to Jerusalem to find their lost twelve-year-old boy. The episode has found its way into many paintings, notably Heinrich Hoffman's *The Finding of Christ in the Temple*. In it, Jesus is depicted standing up and speaking to his elders, who give him their rapt attention. But Luke, the only evangelist to recount the story, writes: "They found him in the temple, sitting among the teachers, listening to them and asking them questions" (Luke 2:46). Hoffman's painting reflects the myriad stories in the apocryphal gospels that never made it into the church canon, stories that portray

Jesus as a kind of Wonder Boy. Personally, I prefer what might be called Luke's Christian understatement: "And Jesus increased in wisdom and in stature, and in favor with God and man" (Luke 2:52). (Or, as we would say today, "with God and his fellow human beings.")

Perhaps it's worth underscoring Jesus' popularity. Some prophets don't become unpopular because they say unpopular things; they are simply unpopular to begin with, and then make the best of the situation; for as we all know, there is more truth squeezed from sour grapes than from all the fruits of success! But according to Luke, people liked Jesus from the beginning. The future Man of Sorrows was probably a boy of joys. He also minded his parents: After describing the episode in the temple, Luke continues, "And he went down with them and came to Nazareth, and was obedient to them" (Luke 2:51).

Of Joseph and Mary's part in the episode, Luke writes, "supposing him to be in the company they went a day's journey, and they sought him among their kinsfolk and acquaintances" (Luke 2:44). It would appear that Joseph and Mary gave their son genuine independence. And what could be more normal than for a mother, having found her lost boy, to burst out: "Son, why have you treated us so? Behold, your father and I have been looking for you anxiously." I'm sure I wouldn't have been half that polite, not after looking for three days! But Jesus, showing amazing independence for a twelve-year-old, answers without a trace of guilt, "Did you not know," or as in the King James version, "Wist ye not that I must be about my father's business?" (Luke 2:49). It's as if Jesus is asking, "I've been with you both for twelve years, and you haven't noticed anything special—how I love to read and argue about Scripture? Have you forgotten that I have a heavenly as well as an earthly father?" It's as if Jesus is saying to Mary, "Like all children, Mom, I'm a loaned treasure. I'm very happy to be on loan to you, but I belong to God who has in mind for me things beyond any you could dream of."

And Mary, bless her heart, doesn't say, "Don't be impertinent," or "Mother knows better," or "Hush your mouth!" No, although she doesn't understand, she keeps an open mind and a good memory. As Luke records, "His mother kept all these things in her heart" (Luke 2:51). How rare is the person who realizes that you can learn more if you don't try to understand too soon. Rarer yet is the parent who can open a discussion without closing it. How rarely parents lead with a light rein, giving their children their heads. And how rare are the children who can voice their expectations for their parents as readily as parents can voice theirs for their children. From this episode we would have to conclude that mother and son are off to a good start.

For the second episode we have to skip eighteen or so years—if, as some scholars believe, Jesus' active ministry began when he was about thirty. At the end of the twelfth chapter of Matthew we read,

While he was still speaking to the people, behold his mother and his brothers stood outside asking to speak to him. But he replied to the man who told him, "Who is my mother? And who are my brothers?" And stretching out his hand toward his disciples he said, "Here are my mother and brothers, for whoever does the will of my Father in heaven is my brother, and my sister, and my mother."

At first hearing, those words certainly have a chilling effect. They seem to bear out Ernest Renan's contention in his *Life of Jesus* that Jesus "warred against the most legitimate cravings of the heart." But suppose we ask what Mary and her sons were doing outside? Why did they call him out to speak to him, and not themselves go in to listen to him? We know that because of his words and deeds, the Pharisees and scribes were after him. We know from the Gospel of John that even his brothers didn't believe in him. And we know from the Gospel of Mark that at one point his friends tried to stop him, thinking he was "beside himself." So it's probably safe to assume that on hearing of his family's arrival, Jesus knew they had come not to open themselves to what he had to say, but rather to persuade him to stop all this radical preaching and come home! Probably Mary wanted to remind him of the backlog of carpentry orders waiting to be filled in Nazareth.

Poor Mary! Your heart has to go out to a mother who keeps hearing such terrible things about her son. But surrendering to her will would have been no answer for Jesus. Had he done what his mother wanted, instead of saving the world, he would have become the best carpenter in Nazareth. It's a familiar story, isn't it, this conflict of visions, these conflicting demands of a heavenly and an earthly parent? If you try seriously to be a child of God, it is almost certain that a protective parent will try to protect you by pleading, "Play it safe, son (or daughter); don't climb out on a limb"—all those protective slogans that become, as it were, the eleventh commandment on which are *hanged* all the law and the prophets! In fact, in the first decades after Jesus' death and resurrection, Christians were so regularly misunderstood by their nearest and dearest that an early martyr exclaimed, "A Christian's only relatives are the saints."

Ponder that, and you can understand better the many seemingly cruel statements of Jesus, statements such as, "He who loves father and mother more than me is not worthy of me" (Matt. 20:37), "It is not peace I have come to bring, but the sword" (Matt. 10:34), or "Let the dead bury the dead" (Matt. 8:22) (which clearly continues, "and not the living"). Put differently: God could not be everywhere and therefore he made mothers, yes—but simply having children doesn't make one a mother. Home is where the heart is, yes—but home can also be a bondage. Jesus understood these family tensions that are so hard on both parents and children. Catch the sorrow in his voice when he says, "A man's enemies will be those in his own household" (Matt. 10:36). And I think he knew how often family tensions take the form of generational conflicts, for he himself said, "I have come to set a man against his father, a daughter against her mother, and a daughter-in-law against her mother-in-law" (Matt. 10:35).

While it is occasionally true that speaking the truth can be an act of hatred, it is generally a grave mistake on the part of children to seek family peace through evasion, repression, and unwarranted compromise (surrendering ethical initiative where none should be surrendered). Earlier I said that Jesus' expectations of his parents were just as legitimate as his parents' expectations of him. Moreover, we should remind ourselves that had all children sought at all costs to avoid all generational conflicts, there might never have been an end to slavery, nor to child labor; there might never have been school integration, an environmental movement, a women's movement, a gay rights or a nuclear freeze movement.

"He who loves father and mother more than me is not worthy of me." Finally, it makes good sense, doesn't it? Harsh, but true.

Let's move on now to the third and last episode. Only at the very end of his life does Jesus finally resolve his conflict with his mother, and then only on a cross: "Mother, here is thy son." And to John, his beloved disciple, he says, "Son, here is thy mother" (John 19:27). That in this moment of agony Jesus could be so filial is deeply moving. Apparently, Mary is widowed, and Jesus is providing for her economic well-being. But he is also looking after her spiritual well-being, and in a very special way. By urging her to join his disciple, Jesus includes her in his mission, and thereby resolves the conflict between his loyalty to her and his loyalty to God.

It is interesting to speculate where Mary's other children might have been, those who had been with her that earlier day outside the synagogue, those brothers to whom a dying son would normally commend his mother. Perhaps they remained in Nazareth, cursing the fool to whom misfortune had related them. But not Mary. What she had suspected in the beginning and doubted in the middle, she finally saw at the end. Clearly, her son had reached her, she is a new person. She is standing, we read, not fainting at the foot of the cross; in distress perhaps too deep for tears, but also in all the legitimate pride of motherhood. And notice that Jesus is not the least bit protective. He doesn't say, "Take her away, John, this is no sight for a mother's eyes to see." No, Mary has to suffer, and then to translate her suffering into the pangs of childbirth that will result in a new and larger family. For Mary will take care not only of John, but of countless others, millions who, in every language of the world, will call her "Mother," because they consider themselves sisters and brothers of Jesus.

Each of us is born of God, as well as of woman. Each of us, whether we be parents or children, has dual citizenship, here below and in the City of God. Each of us has dual parentage with our earthly parents and our heavenly Father/Mother. Each of us has dual membership in our family and in the world, that larger family so desperately in need of the beautiful love we see in the relationship of Mary and Jesus, mother and son.

# 17. Fire or Fire

Reading: Acts 2:1–21, 43–47

The other day I saw this cartoon: A man who had apparently just entered an office peered across and down the other side of a desk and said to another man, who was lying on his back on the floor, "Look, Gormly, there is such a thing as being too laid-back." I say "Amen" to the cartoon and its insight. Another example: Last Sunday afternoon I saw a young man in the park seated on a bench. At his side was an apparition of delight and on his knee a pocket calculator. As I passed, I heard him say, "How do I love thee? Let me count the ways." That man confirmed a deep-seated suspicion that it's no more than a hop, skip, and a jump from "cool and laid-back" to "dead and buried."

In any event, today, of all days, is not one to be cool and laid-back, because this Sunday we celebrate the day of the fiery Pentecost. Don't ask exactly what happened on that day, fifty days after Christ's resurrection, for no one knows for sure. Once again, as it is so often the case in the Bible, it is the invisible event that counts. We know only that the eleven disciples, heretofore waiting and watching for God, began to be used and moved by God. After Pentecost they became ten times the people they were during Jesus' life on earth. And because of the demonstrated power of the Holy Spirit moving through Peter and the other disciples—witness, three thousand converted in one day—Pentecost is widely considered the birthday of the Church.

That's important. For if it is the coming of the Spirit that marks the beginning of the Christian Church, then to Christians the integrity of love should be much more important than the purity of dogma. If the Church was founded on a day when Peter stood up to speak with a loud voice of the sun turning into darkness and the moon into blood, and exhorted his hearers, "Save yourself from this crooked generation" (Acts 2:40), then Christians have no business thinking that the good life consists mainly in not doing bad things. We have no business thinking that to do evil in this world you have to be a Bengal tiger, when, in fact, it is enough to be a tame tabby— a nice person but not a good one. In short, Pentecost makes it clear that nothing is so fatal to Christianity as indifference. The true infidels are the truly indifferent, the cool and laid back, the spiritually dead and buried. You may remember what Ernest Hemingway wrote of Francis Macomber: "He always had a great tolerance which seemed the nicest thing about him, if it were not the most sinister."

In his first letter to the Corinthians, Paul writes, "The Kingdom of God consists not in words, but in power" (1 Cor. 4:20). That's what comes through most of all on that first day of Pentecost. Peter spoke words, lots of them, good ones, too; but what clearly cut to the heart of his hearers was the power of the Holy Spirit working through him. Peter energized his hearers, he fired up, like a furnace, their imaginations. He quickened their hearts, and made their spirits soar sufficiently to make them stand against the blandishments of the crooked generation into which they were born.

"The Kingdom of God consists not in words, but in power." There's a story told of Heinrich Heine. The German-Jewish poet was standing with a friend before the great cathedral of Amiens. When the friend asked, "Why can't people build piles like this anymore?" Heine replied, "My dear friend, in those days people had convictions. We moderns have opinions, and it takes more than opinions to build a gothic cathedral."

Likewise, it takes more than opinions to build Christian communities. What it takes is the same energy, ignited imagination, the same courage born of conviction—all fruits of the

Holy Spirit—that once poured forth in such abundance on Peter and the disciples. For let us not take refuge in mindless optimism; our times are no less perverse than theirs. So to us, as to Peter's hearers, comes his exhortation: "Save yourselves from this crooked generation."

Several years ago John Gardner, founder of Common Cause and hardly a wild-eyed radical, wrote of his country, "The nation disintegrates. I use the phrase soberly, the nation disintegrates." Would he feel differently today? I doubt it, for ghettoes, once considered problems, are today, in effect, solutions. The same is true of prisons. Prisons, ghettoes—that's where we put the expendable of our society. Ours, as John Kenneth Galbraith recently termed it, is a "heartless society"; one in which to an extraordinary degree, "the fortunate have managed to get the impoverished out of their thoughts and off their consciences."

It is interesting to recall that in 1946, immediately after World War II, when this nation was at the pinnacle of its power, our leading playwright, Eugene O'Neill, explained in the course of a *New York Times* interview, that he "worked on the theory that the United States, instead of being the most successful country in the world, is the greatest failure. Its main idea is that everlasting game of trying to possess your own soul by possession of something outside it." He said that we were "the clearest example of 'For what shall it profit a man if he gain the whole world and lose his own soul.' ".

Recently, a minister friend of mine took an East German pastor on a tour around New York City. Impressed by the extremes of affluence and poverty that he saw, the East German said quietly to my friend, "You know that I am not a Communist. But New York City would make me one."

" . . . that everlasting game of trying to possess your own soul by possession of something outside it." In any country, wherever there are riches and power the game is played and souls are lost. This is true even in the churches, where too often ministers and lay leaders are eager for power—not to share it, but to possess it, not to create with it, but to exercise it by saying "No" to almost every creative idea that comes along.

So on this day of Pentecost, this nineteen hundred and something birthday of the Christian Church, let me suggest the following: Remembering, from Peter's words that the Holy Spirit is a discomforter as well as comforter, let us not fear the "cleansing" fire of Pentecost. Who was it who said, "Truth is error burnt up?" Certainly, truth is only possible when our make-believe world lies in ashes. Therefore, as regards our personal lives, let us pray mightily to God to pour down upon us the Holy Spirit, whose power can overturn our beloved self-protecting lies, whose power can say "No" to the secret flatterings of self-importance, and pull the rug from under ambition's tower of blocks.

Then let us pray that the Holy Spirit in this and every church makes of us a community of believers like unto the one formed in Jerusalem on that first day of Pentecost. May we speak in many tongues the one message of Christ's love for us and all humanity. May we see to it that the cruelty and greed we see around us find no place among us. And when in the world we side, as side we must, with the oppressed against the oppressor, may we do so with the clear understanding that if, by God's grace, the Holy Spirit is alive in us, it needs only liberation in those we oppose.

Sisters and brothers, the whole world disintegrates. And we're not going to save it by being cool and laid-back. Nor are we going to save it by opinions, not even the right opinions of the Church. Nor certainly are we going to save it by continuing to play the everlasting game of trying to possess our souls by trying to possess something outside them. In this nuclear age, which threatens to turn every man, woman, and child into a nuclear ash, it is clearer now than ever that only God's heavenly fire, moving and using us, can contain the ever-advancing flames of hell. Playwrights, poets, they generally say it best:

The dove descending breaks the air
With flame of incandescent terror,
Of which the tongues declare
The sole discharge of sin and error.
Our only hope, or else despair,
Lies in the choice of pyre or pyre,
To be consumed by fire or fire.

(T. S. Eliot, *Four Quartets*)

# 18. Nature and Nature's God*

Thus says the Lord
who gives the sun for light by day
and the fixed order of the moon
and the stars for light by night,
who stirs up the seas so that its waves roar—
the Lord of hosts is His name:
"If this fixed order departs
before me," says the Lord,
"then shall the descendants of Israel cease
from being a nation before me for ever."
Thus says the Lord:
"If the heavens above can be measured,
and the foundations of the earth below can be explored,
then I will cast off all the descendants of Israel
for all that they have done," says the Lord.

(Jeremiah 31:35–37)

Once upon a time the university and church were wed. Then they were divorced, the university pleading mental cruelty. And the university was right. Not the great theologians, nor the great musicians, nor the great artists, but the little inquisitors of Europe and the little inquisitors of Puritan America were diminishing and deadening life. They were guilty of what psychiatrists call, in a nice phrase, "premature closure." They wanted order, but at the expense of splendor. They wanted to help; but like most people in power they would rather be responsible for, than responsive to, the people they wanted to help. Most of all, I think they wanted control.

---

* This sermon is about ecology, the church, and the university, and for it I owe a great debt of thanks to Theodore Roszak's *Where the Wasteland Ends: Politics and Transcendence in Post-Industrial Society* (New York: Doubleday, 1972).

No wonder then that Newton and Galileo and Francis Bacon cried out "more room!" These first scientists of the Enlightenment and their philosophic champions were not atheists, they weren't even anti-ecclesiastical. And they were not, in idolatrous fashion, worshiping their new-found scientific methodology. On the contrary, the new methodology was to serve ancient and high purposes—to combat ignorance and superstition, to release the bottled-up genie of imaginative human energy. Bacon, I imagine, would have agreed with the prediction of the later philosopher Joseph Ernest Renan: "The main contribution of science will be to deliver us from superstition, not to reveal ultimate truth."

We can catch all these strains in the preface to the second edition of Newton's great *Principia Mathematica*, written by Robert Coates.

The gates are now set open, and by the passage Newton has revealed we may freely enter into the hidden secrets and wonders of natural things. . . . Therefore, we may now more nearly behold the beauties of Nature, and entertain ourselves with the delightful contemplation; and, which is the best and most valuable fruit of philosophy, be thence incited the more profoundly to reverence and adore the great Maker and Lord of all. He must be blind who from the wisest and most excellent contrivances of things cannot see the infinite wisdom and goodness of their almighty Creator, and he must be mad and senseless who refuses to acknowledge them.

Mr. Coates, I imagine, would find a lot of us mad and senseless. But let us not denounce the godless; rather, let us ask, "Where has all the grandeur gone?" Why is it that the descendants of the Enlightenment seem to be walking in gross darkness? Why is it that students are today deeply alienated? Could it be that the University is now diminishing and deadening life, bottling up the genie of imaginative energies, putting on all of us what William Blake once called "mind-forged manacles"?

I think we can trace an important progression from the Enlightenment to now. Newton, Galileo, and Bacon did not separate Nature from Nature's God. But their successors quickly did, and the divorce left Nature without any animating purpose. Nature still held its beauty, but the greedy eyes of human beings focused more on the riches in the warehouse than on the beauty in the shop. "We shall become the masters and possessors of Nature," said René Descartes. So a qualitative view of Nature gradually gave way to a quantitative view. Nature was seen as neutral, essentially a machine. And a machine has no purpose, only a function. It was obvious that Nature's function was to serve us human beings, the only purposeful creatures around. So over the centuries, as Descartes had predicted, human beings have become powerful, mastering and possessing Nature.

But power is purchased at the expense of communion. (That's why love is self-restricting when it comes to power.) If, for instance, you want to dominate natives, as in colonialism, you cannot communicate with them. If you want to dominate emotions, as in Victorianism, you cannot communicate with your emotions. In other words, if to know means to dominate and objectify, then the very act of knowing becomes an act of alienation. That's why there is so little humility in the academic world, and so little love in this kind of knowledge. And imagination and vision are rarely called upon. (Love is not blind but visionary.)

So e.e. cummings wrote:

> I would rather learn from one bird how to sing
> Than teach ten thousand stars how not to dance.

So William Blake vigorously opposed what he called the "single vision" of scientific methodology, and wrote on the title page of *Vala* these words of St. Paul: "For we contend not with flesh and blood, but with dominion and authority, with the world ruling powers of this dark age, with the spirit of evil in heavenly places" (Eph. 6:12).

Blake foresaw that scientific methodology, once a servant at the service of loving masters, would become a loveless master, a "world-ruling power in this dark age." Blake was prophetic, for the scientific method has won us over, lock, stock, and barrel, to its conception of truth. Do you want to know what's real? It's what's objectively real. Do you want to know how this butterfly works? Tear the wings off. Analyze the parts. Get down to the hard facts.

Of course, there are still some good old human values lying around, but they are worn like a faded flower in the lapel of hard facts. So the Progression from the Enlightenment to this day goes like this: Once the stars were seen as parts of a machine, it was only a step—a psychological step—to view animals as machines, as did Descartes; then to view human society as a machine, as did Hobbes; to view the human body as a machine, as did La Mettrie; to view human behavior as machinelike, as did Pavlov, Watson, and most recently and notoriously B. F. Skinner. And need we add that if you can objectify and depersonalize human beings under a microscope, you can do it the more easily under a bombsight.

Charles Gillespie said, "The scientific act of knowing is an act of alienation." It seems to me that as long as political scientists and sociologists and philosophers and literary critics, yes even teachers of the faith—as long as all these non-scientists take their standard of intellectual respectability primarily from the sciences, as long as they believe that the objective route is the only respectable access to reality, then every act of knowing will be an act of alienation. The more we objectify knowledge, the more, as Theodore Roszak says, "We force experience out and away from our personal grip."

Let us make a mean remark just to be provocative. Most professors don't want to visit the place, they'd rather read the map. It is not the experience that's real, it's the explanation of the experience.

From whence come the mind-forged manacles of today? From the drive to objectify, to depersonalize, which stems, once again, from premature closure. Again, it is the drive for order at the sake of splendor. We are contending with a "more objective than thou complex," and I say "complex" advisedly, for the objective mode of consciousness pushed to the extreme is a psychological rather than an epistomological stance. The objective mode of consciousness has more to do with a way of feeling—or of not feeling—than with a way of knowing. To be "tough-minded" spares us the vulnerability that comes of being tenderhearted. It allows us the more easily to master, to dominate, to control—and deem unimportant what cannot be mastered, dominated, and controlled.

Where the churches were once the great promoters of petty orthodoxy, now it is the universities. Knowledge for power at the expense of love and humility. (Where does the heart go to school in higher education?)

It is small wonder, then, that so many students feel that under the academic hand life has been diminished and deadened. For to view life impersonally is to see life that is shallow, unexperienced, academic; and in this way of looking there is finally more blindness than seeing.

"Circumcise yourselves to the Lord, remove the foreskin of your hearts," says Jeremiah (Jer. 4:4). The Bible does not enjoin us to be tender-minded, but it does insist that we be tenderhearted. The Bible does not claim that faith is a substitute for thought. It insists that faith is what makes good thinking possible—something the Roman Catholic Church recognized when it made the first cardinal virtue *prudentia*, which basically means good thinking.

But back to the text now, which is perhaps beginning to make more sense.

Thus says the Lord who gives the sun for light by day and the fixed order of the moon and the stars for light by night . . . If this fixed order departs from before me, says the Lord, then shall the descendants of Israel cease from being a nation. . . . If the heavens above can be measured, and the foundations of the earth below can be explored, then I will cast off all the descendants of Israel for all that they have done. (Jer. 31:35–37)

In a last-ditch effort to save the world from complete depersonalization, most secular humanists today set up two cultures—one for things and one for persons. According to this scheme things can be known rationally, but human beings cannot. Human beings cannot be objectified and dissected without being destroyed. Human beings are a mystery, and hence our deepest knowledge of human beings comes through communion. Communion is possible, for there is something in each of us that we can recognize in our neighbors.

Good luck! As Theodore Roszak points out, while the intention is noble, "it is apt to cut no ice with the hardnosed behaviorists who will wonder why this particular conglomeration of molecules and atoms and electrochemical circuitry called a human being should indeed be regarded as different, special, unique."

Therefore, instead of trying to defend against the encroachments of the objective mode, what about trying to expand the area of subjectivity, to expand the mode of subjective consciousness? Suppose for a moment that we might find some mysterious deep kinship not only with each other, but with animals and flowers, with all of Nature? Suppose we were to re-wed Nature to Nature's God?

It is at this point that ecologists have made their most profound contributions. For while some ecologists are merely asking for caution, lest we exhaust our natural resources and kill ourselves in the process, others are asking for reverence. And why reverence? Because nature has animating purposes of its own.

These ecologists are threatening to many academics. Here's a paragraph on ecology in the latest Encyclopedia Britannica:

The wholistic emphasis implied by the very idea of human ecology has been a continual threat to the unity of the discipline. Comprehensive treatises on the subject typically represented expressions of social philosophy rather than empirically grounded statements of scientific theory. Indeed, numerous commentators have put forth the view that human ecology must remain a philosophic view point rather than aspire to the status of a systematic discipline.

Catch that "aspire to the status!"

Now let's read another statement on ecology, this time from Roszak:

Among the Iroquois the bear was highly esteemed. When the hunted bear was confronted, the kill was preceded by a long monologue in which the needs of the hunter were fully explained, and assurances were given that the killing was motivated by need and not by a wish to dishonor. [It is a bit difficult to picture the bear waiting around all this time, but what's being said is very important and very beautiful!] The hunter who believes that all matter and actions are sacramental and consequential will bring deference and understanding to his relations with the environment. He will achieve a steady state with his environment; he will live in harmony with Nature and survive because of it.

Now I think we can understand the text. Jeremiah is telling us that once Nature is separated from Nature's God, the whole human structure will begin to collapse. Perhaps this is a word not only ecologists, but the Church might gently whisper to the University. Certainly if we wish to know not only more, but to know deeper, we shall need more love and humility and communion. And I dare say it might even be more fun to "learn from one bird how to sing than to teach ten thousand stars how not to dance."

# 19. "Sail On, O Ship of State"

Reading: Matthew 14:22–33

What if modern scholarship should one day establish that the silver dollar George Washington hurled across the mighty Rappahannock had, in fact, splashed? Would George Washington still remain, as we were taught in grammar school, "first in war, first in peace, first in the hearts of his countrymen?" The answer, of course, is "Yes"; for the story of the silver dollar is an expression of faith, not a basis of faith. It is the kind of story followers of George Washington, committed to him on other grounds, would love to tell of him—around a good campfire.

Likewise, if Jesus never walked on the Sea of Galilee, he is still to Christians their Messiah. For Christ is not God's magic incarnate, but God's love incarnate. He was not one to go around—Houdini-like—breaking the laws of physical nature; but rather one who, beyond all limits of human nature, loved as none before nor after him has ever loved. In the face of such awesome love even the waves must rise up and the winds bow down, even as at his birth a star stood still, and at his death the earth quaked, rending rocks and splitting graves wide open.

And what is the meaning of the story? Ask a crowd straining their necks to see what's on the ceiling of the Sistine Chapel what they find there, or ask an audience listening to Beethoven's Ninth Symphony what they are hearing, and no two answers will be the same. Such is the evocative power of great works of art. As biblical stories stimulate even more the imagination, no one should be surprised that I see in this story a perfect three-act drama for a Fourth of July sermon.

As the first act opens, the disciples are boarding a boat for what appears to be a routine crossing. But, at some distance from the shore, they find themselves buffeted by an unexpected and terrible storm. Their boat begins to sink; and not only because the winds are high and against them, but also, as it turns out, because Jesus is not there.

Well, were we not also taught in grammar school: "Thou too sail on, O Ship of State,/ Sail on, O Union strong and great"? And in the middle of World War II, didn't Churchill send Roosevelt a morale-building telegram quoting that Longfellow poem more fully:

> Thou too sail on, O Ship of State,
> Sail on, O Union strong and great.
> Humanity with all its fears,
> With all the hopes of future years,
> Is hanging breathless on thy fate . . .

But nobody sends us telegrams like that any more. We too seem at sea, caught in a storm with no compass to point us toward a promising future. That we've come a long way, there's no denying. Even though we were a white nation founded on the genocide and bondage of other races; and though we've a long way to go in our treatment of blacks and Native Americans, ethnic minorities and women (what's one woman on the Supreme Court but hollow symbolism when death comes to the Equal Rights Amendment?); still, ours is the longest-lasting revolution in the world, over two hundred years old. And the liberties established way back then, in a remote agrarian backwater, have miraculously survived and at times positively flourished.

But today something has happened to our understanding of freedom, to our notion of democracy. Our eighteenth-century forebears were enormously influenced by Montesquieu, the French thinker who differentiated despotism, monarchy, and democracy. In each he found a special principle governing social life. For despotism that principle was fear, for monarchy

honor, and for democracy—take heed!—virtue. "It is this qual-
ity," he wrote, "rather than fear or ambition, that makes things
work in a democracy."

Samuel Adams agreed: "We may look to armies for our
defense, but virtue is our best security. It is not possible that
any state should long remain free where virtue is not su-
premely honored."

Freedom, virtue—these two were practically synonymous in
the minds of our revolutionary forebears. To them it was in-
conceivable that an individual would be granted freedom merely
for the satisfaction of instincts and whims. Freedom, virtue—
they were still practically synonymous a hundred years later
in the mind of Abraham Lincoln when in his Second Inaugural
Address he called for "a new birth of freedom." Freedom and
virtue seem to embrace one another in perhaps the greatest of
all American hymns, written by Julia Ward Howe:

> In the beauty of the lilies Christ was born across the sea,
> With a glory in his bosom that transfigures you and me;
> As he died to make men holy, let us die to make men free!
> While God is marching on.

Today we Americans are not marching in the ways of the
Lord, but limping along in our own ways, thinking not of the
public weal but of our private interests. Today tax-cutting is
more popular than social spending, even for the poorest Americans. And because we have so cruelly separated freedom from
virtue—because we define freedom in a morally inferior way—
our "Union strong and great" is stalled in a storm, in what
Herman Melville called the "Dark Ages of Democracy," a time
when, as he predicted, the New Jersualem would turn into
Babylon, and Americans would feel "the arrest of hope's ad-
vance." America today is a cross between a warship and a
luxury liner, with all attention concentrated on the upper decks.
But below the water line there are leaks. Our ship is sinking.

But on to Act II, which opens with one person preparing to
abandon ship. And can't you hear the cries—there are so

many of them in every sinking ship: "For God's sake, Peter, sit down—you're rocking the boat!"

What do you suppose moved Peter, and not the others, to abandon ship? To most human beings there is something fundamentally unacceptable about unpleasant truth. Most of the time we seek to bolster our illusions, to protect ourselves from our fears. But in our more courageous and honest moments, some of us are willing to face the shallowness of our personal relations, the barbaric ladders on which we climb to success, the banality of our culture, the cruelty in our foreign policy. And when in the fourth watch of the night—that miserable 2 A.M. to 6 A.M. shift when we are most alone with ourselves—Jesus bids us come, some of us—like Peter—are ready for that leap of faith.

Peter almost immediately begins to sink, and modern scholarship may one day establish that Jesus called him "the Rock" then, not for his foundational but for his sinking properties! And why not? "In my weakness is my strength," said St. Paul (2 Cor. 12:10), who had the vision to see that "God's power is made perfect in weakness" (2 Cor. 12:9). It is only when we realize that we can no more trust our own buoyancy than we can that of the ship we have just abandoned, that we truly give ourselves to Christ. Then the true miracle takes place, the one that makes this story eternally, if not literally true. "Lord, save me," cries Peter, and Jesus does (Matt. 14:31). There's the central miracle of every Christian life, which should take place on an average of about every other day. When, sinking in our sense of helplessness, we reach out for a love greater than we ourselves can ever express, when we reach out for a truth deeper than we could ever articulate, and for a beauty richer than we ourselves can ever contain—when we too cry out "Lord, save me," he who died to make us holy does indeed transfigure you and me. Cry out for a thimbleful of help and you receive an oceanful in return.

Many people wish the story ended here. What greater relief to an unhappy soul than to find stability in a world of turmoil, certitude in a world of doubt, contentment amid pain? But the goal of the Christian life is not to save your soul but to transcend yourself, to vindicate the human struggle of which all of us are a part, to keep hope advancing. Peter doesn't say to Jesus, "Now that you have saved me, Lord, let's walk off— just you and me—into the sunrise of a new day and forget all about those fellows in the sinking ship." No, having abandoned the sinking ship for Jesus, Peter now returns with Jesus.

There is our Fourth of July message, our Fourth of July example for patriots who call themselves Christians: "America, love it *and* leave it." Leave it for Jesus, for America's sake as well as your own, and then return with Jesus. That's how to love America—with Christ's wisdom, with Christ's compassion, with a concern for the whole, fusing once again freedom with virtue in order to renew "the patriot's dream, that sees beyond the years, her alabaster cities gleam, undimmed by human tears."

When Peter returned to the boat with Jesus, the winds abated. I think our own ship could once again recover headway and direction if only American Christians followed Peter's example. With faith in God, it's right to love one's country, love it as Jesus did Israel.

Longfellow may have been a bit triumphant in his view of America, but he was right in the fervor of his love. These are the more prayerful words he addressed to our nation at the end of his poem:

> Sail on, nor fear to breast the sea.
> Our hearts, our hopes are all with thee,
> Our hearts, our hopes, our prayers, our tears,
> Our faith triumphant o'er our fears,
> Are all with thee, are all with thee.

# 20. Young Abraham

Reading: Genesis 12:1–9

By faith Abraham obeyed the call to go out to a land destined for himself and his heirs and left home without knowing where he was to go. (Hebrews 11:8)

At seventy-five, Abraham is no spring chicken; and with all his possessions and descendants along, he's not exactly traveling light. How many of us half his age would be so willing to pull up stakes and take off for parts unknown? And can't you hear the townsfolk in Haran?

"What is this, Abraham, some wild dream?"

"Look, the future isn't what it used to be, particularly when you don't know where in the world you're going."

"Have you talked this out with Sarah?"

"What about that promising nephew of yours, Lot, who was valedictorian last year in the school—is this fair to him?"

"More than your humility would probably realize, Abraham, to all of us here in Haran you've become indispensable."

To the last observation Abraham gave one of the best answers of this life. It is not recorded in Genesis, but I happen to know it. He said, "No one is indispensable, except to God."

No one is indispensable, except to God. Dig that one out of your eyes, mothers and fathers! How do you like that, employers and ministers! Sure, they need us—our children, our employees, our parishioners—but not that badly. No one is indispensable—except to God. And why to God? Because God is the eternal Creator, who needs every one of us to continue creation's work. God wants to make humanity more human, so God wants each of us to protect, affirm, dignify life—more and more of it.

When you stop to think of it, who should be better suited to further the work of Creation than elders like Abraham? More than younger people, elders use their memories—and memory, as Frederick Buechner says in *Now and Then*, "is more than a looking back at a time that is no longer; it is looking out into another kind of time altogether where everything that was continues not just to be, but to grow and change with the life that is in it still." Memory is something like a running broad jump: It takes you back, the further to launch you forward. Rightly lived, then, as Abraham lived them, the senior years should be the formative years. Old age is dying young as late as possible. Like Abraham, elders should look out and see and respond to the life that still needs to be protected, affirmed, dignified. If they look back, it should be primarily to remember, as did Abraham, who they were created to be— God's guiltless, cared-for, and caring children, called to be co-creators with the Creator.

The story of Abraham is a powerful one in a country like ours, where over 2 million citizens a year turn 65, bringing the grand total of those over 65 to upward of 25 million. From 1900 to 1984 life expectancy increased from 49 to 74.5 years. And today science and daily experience are continually destroying the myths of aging. Senility is not a sign of age; it is a sign of a disease. Senility, dementia, Alzheimer's disease— call it what you will—someday, like cancer, scientists will understand and cure it. Like racism and sexism, ageism is shot full of lies. Only a fraction of "OPs" (as demographers affectionately refer to old people) are severely disabled. In short, the expectation of decline becomes a self-fulfilling prophesy. Do not judge by appearances: Any OP who remains socially involved, mentally active, with a personality flexible enough to tolerate ambiguity and to enjoy new experiences can pull up stakes and take off for parts unknown as did Abraham, if and when God calls him or her to do so.

All this should be music to old ears, and to young ones too, for what could be worse than to reach seventy, look back to the springtime of your life and say, "Ah, those were the days!"— and be right!

Robert Browning had the right idea:

> Grow old along with me
> The best is yet to be
> The last of life
> For which the first was made.
> Our times are in his hand
> Who said, "A whole I planned."
> Trust God, see all, nor be afraid.

The story of any one of us is in some measure the story of all of us. This makes Abraham's story ours, be we old or young. It tells us that if we think we have no choice we've made the wrong choice. If we think we're too old or too young to choose, we're wrong again. Abraham would agree with Karl Barth: "Better something doubtful or overbold, and therefore in need of forgiveness, than nothing at all." (I was once introduced as one who would rather ask for forgiveness than seek permission. I took it as a compliment!)

There's a Yiddish story about a man to whom all kinds of misfortunes befell. When he pleaded with the Lord, "Why me, I who have so consistently and conscientiously fulfilled everyone of the 613 laws of the Pentateuch?" a still, small voice from heaven replied, "Because you're a 'noodge'—a bore." I'm sure God would rather we were creative than right! In my office is a poster that reads: "Do not follow where the path leads. Rather go where there is no path and leave a trail."

Think for a moment of the American trailblazers among America's suffragettes, many of whose faces were as full as Abraham's of the "credentials of humanity," as Shaw once called wrinkles. For a century and a half we American men excluded an entire sex from governing what we liked to call the greatest democracy of the world. Only sixty-odd years ago did women win the right to vote. Then, for years, almost all wives voted as did their husbands. (Don't protest. My mother did and I'll bet most of your mothers did the same!) But today there is a recognizable gender gap on a variety of issues that still reflect the values and practices imposed by a white male power structure that still controls both the economy and the government. What an explosion of needs, self-discoveries, and new insights into personal and social relationships we men owe to those feminists who in their time, like Abraham and Sarah before them, chose not to follow where the paths of their day led. Rather, they went where there were no paths and left a remarkable trail.

God is constantly trying to make humanity more human. Too often we picture God as an immoveable rock when, in fact, it is God and God alone who refuses to rest. I only quote Scripture: "He neither slumbers not sleeps" (Ps. 123) and "Behold I create all things new" (Rev. 21:5). Surely God's most persistent enemies must be those unwilling to move in new directions. "Better something doubtful or overbold, and therefore in need for forgiveness, than nothing at all." Yes, if you choose, you're sometimes wrong; but if you never choose, you're always wrong.

Of course you don't have to move out, as did Abraham, to respond to God's call to be creative. You can be born again— and again—in place. Christians are born of the water, symbol of forgiveness, and of the spirit, symbol of power. When I make hospital calls and see people fighting for their lives, and their relatives struggling to stay alive spiritually, I am astounded at what we human beings can do if we have to. In fact, what we can do if we have to is matched only by what we don't do if we think we don't have to. But Christians have to, baptized as we are by the water and by the spirit. Whatever our age, whatever our station, we can be constant in faithfulness—that is, creativity. We can help God make humanity more human.

Abraham lived through "summer's parching heat," and

Jesus died young. But didn't both of them demonstrate that it is by its content rather than its duration that a lifetime is measured? So let us like Abraham, and with our Risen Lord, be co-creators with the Creator who saith, "A whole I planned."

It's really easy. You have only to "trust God, see all, nor be afraid."

# 21. In Praise of Rest

God rested on the seventh day and hallowed it, because on it God rested from all his work. (Genesis 2:3)

There's more than a little sadness to what Labor Day weekend signals to many of us—vacation's end. But before praising the virtues of August and rest, I want first to sympathize with those who have long been on forced vacations by virtue of having been laid off work. It is important to remember that unemployment is a social failure rather than a personal one. It is a public scandal, as well as a personal tragedy. It is my hope that this nation will soon awake to see that the right to work, like the right to food, is a moral right and thence deserves the same legal protection we today accord freedom of speech, of the press, and of religion.

And one more thing. If you are unemployed, you are probably suffering an identity crisis—which, in some measure, is always a religious crisis. So please, be like a nail: The harder unemployment hits you, the deeper let it drive you into the everlasting arms of the only one to whom you should accord power to tell you who you are. On welfare or off, with or without unemployment compensation, you are God's precious daughter or son, and don't let unemployment tell you differently.

Now back to the text that calls to remembrance that first sabbath when, after six days of wild creativity, God took a day off to catch her breath.

Notice that God did not hallow the day on which God made "the beasts of the earth, the birds of the air, the fish of the sea, and every creeping thing that creeps upon the earth." God did not hallow even that day in which she made you and me, "male and female" (Gen. 2:3). No, God hallowed that day only on which God did nothing at all but rest. It makes me think there must be more to this business of resting than meets the eye.

In summertime in New York City, I love to walk in Riverside Park. For one thing, it's the most noncompetitive scene in the city. With the exception of purse-snatchers and an occasional mean child, no one is trying to take anything from anybody; and only on a see-saw is someone trying to rise by making someone else go down. And everybody—those reading on the benches, the dog walkers, the frisbee players, the lovers strolling down the paths, and the families sitting on the grass or on gaily colored blankets—everyone is receiving something. What they are receiving is a renewed sense of physical and spiritual well-being. It's coming from everywhere: from the sky and air, from clouds and singing birds; from the sounds of the Riverside carillon and the sight of the Circle Line ferry coming down the Hudson River on the home stretch of what has to be one of the most spectacular trips any tourist could take around any city in this world. But most of all, this sense of well-being is coming from the folks themselves, from each other, because they have time now, for each other. And with the exception of the ice cream cones, it's all free! "Lord, of thy fulness have we received, grace upon grace."

If on the seventh day God needed to rest, you can count on it, so do we. Our sputtering hearts, our reeling heads, our dragging feet, from time to time they all need to receive anew that sense of well-being. It's dangerous theology to think you can improve on God. As a matter of fact, there is something prideful about our reluctance to rest more often. Sometimes it is more blessed to receive than to give; at least it takes more humility.

I imagine on that first Sabbath, with all she had to celebrate, God threw a party for herself. You think I'm joking, but read the fifteenth chapter of Luke and you will find the following: At the end of the parable of the lost sheep, when the sheep was found, the shepherd threw a party; at the end of the parable of the lost coin, when the coin was found the woman threw a party; and at the end of the parable of the prodigal son, when the son was found, the father threw a party. According to Jesus, God is partying all the time, and—once again—it's dangerous theology to think you can improve on God.

God rested, and God threw a party. I imagine God also took stock. She had a lot to think about, and so do we. The other day in the park, I passed a person on a bench reading Barbara Tuchman's *Guns of August*. It occurred to me that to go to another place (the park), and to another time (the first decade of our century), was a wonderful way to triangulate in on yourself and your own time. "Am I being what I really want to be, doing what I really want to do? Is my church doing all it can to make Christ visible? What more could my nation do about the violence of American life so dreadfully apparent in marginal and expendable people out of work and on welfare?"

Also, "How fares my relationship with God?" Years after the death of Gertrude Stein, her constant companion, Alice Toklas, said of her a wonderful thing: "It wasn't what Gertrude gave me, which was so much, it was what she never took away." I often think of God that way. What impresses me is not only what God gives, but what God never takes away. Put differently, it's a wonderful thing to be loved by someone who is never in competition with you, someone who wants only your well-being. God is that person, the only person in your life who will never compete with you. That is why it is so restful to be with God, and why God is so readily found in rest. "Be still, and know that I am God" (Ps. 46:10). "Come unto me, all ye who labor and are heavy laden, and I will give you rest" (Matt. 11:28).

As God will never compete with us, so she will never desert us. Many of you, probably, know the hymn "O love, that wilt not let me go—". What you may not know is that it was written by George Matheson, the famous Scotch theologian/preacher, who in his handsome youth was engaged to a beautiful woman. When the doctors determined that Matheson was going blind, she broke the engagement. It was then, in the depths of grief, that he sat down and poured out:

> O love, that wilt not let me go,
> I rest my weary soul in thee.
> I give thee back the life I owe;
> That in thine ocean depth its flow
> May richer, fuller be.

O lovers, never forget that love is greater than the sum of its hearts!

A final purpose to rest seems obvious this Labor Day weekend: to return us to work. Although God rested on the seventh day, there is certainly no indication that that was what God had in mind to do forever and ever. It certainly wasn't long before rescuing the human race became a full-time job. (God has had many problems, but unemployment has not been one of them!) And saving the human race—quite literally—is our job too, our most urgent task. Success is far from guaranteed, but if we can't be optimistic, we can be persistent. If we rest with God, we can also return with God, in words of St. Paul (2 Tim. 4:7), "to run the straight race, to fight the good fight, to endure unto the end," until with all the saints, "who from their labors rest," we are made partakers of God's eternal kingdom.

# 22. Death Is More Friend Than Foe

Reading: Romans 8:31–37

I want to talk about death, but not because I am feeling morbid, sad, or even old. "Old" to me is when you get into your rocking chair and have trouble getting it started. "Old" is when you get winded playing checkers. "Old" is when the only glint in your eye comes from the sun hitting your trifocals just right. No, I want to talk of death because it is good, from time to time, to contemplate the end towards which, with irreversible steps, we all walk.

Let us take as a text three words of Paul found in 1 Corinthians 13:8, "Love never ends." Love feels just like that, doesn't it? Love feels like it's forever. And because love refuses to be imprisoned by time, when someone we love dies, grief renders everything unreal. But when unbearable grief becomes bearable sorrow, we can profitably meditate on certain truths about death.

In the first place, death is not the enemy we generally make it out to be. Consider only the alternative, life without death. Life without death would be interminable—literally, figuratively. We'd take days just to get out of bed, weeks to decide what to do next. Students would never graduate, and faculty meetings, deacon meetings, and all kinds of other meetings would go on for months. Chances are, we'd be as bored as the ancient Greek gods and up to their same silly tricks. Death cannot be the enemy if it is death that brings us to life. You see what I'm after: just as without leave-taking, there can be no arrival; just as without a growing old, there can be no growing up; just as without tears, no laughter; so without death, there could be no living. So let us pause to thank, with brief thanksgiving, our Creator who so organized things that "all mortal flesh is as the grass" (Prov. 40:6).

Death enhances not only our individual life, but our common life as well. Death *is* the great equalizer—not because death makes us equal, but because death mocks our pretentions at being anything else. In the face of death, all differences of race and class and nationality become known for the trivial things they ultimately are. I love the old Moravian cemeteries, which house no pyramids to the ego, all tombstones being flat; and when Mrs. Schmidt dies, her final resting place is next to the person who died just before her in the community. What a wonderful thing it would be if the structure of Moravian cemeteries could also influence our communal life!

I recently learned something else about death, something quite wonderful and unexpected. In Arthur Miller's play *After the Fall*, one of the characters cries out, "Good God, why is betrayal the only truth that sticks?" That's a truth that most of us know well! What I hadn't known was that death has a way with grievances, a way quite wonderfully described in a sonnet of John Greenleaf Whittier's called "Forgiveness":

> My heart was heavy, for its trust had been
> Abused, its kindness answered with foul wrong:
> So, turning gloomily from my fellow-men,
> One summer Sabbath-day, I strolled among
> The green mounds of the village burial place;
> Where pondering how all human love and hate
> Find one sad level, and how, soon or late,
> Wronged and wrongdoer, each with meekened face,
> And cold hands folded over a still heart,
> Pass the green threshold of our common grave,
> Whither all footsteps tend, whence none depart,
> Awed for myself and pitying my race,
> Our common sorrow, like a mighty wave,
> Swept all my pride away, and trembling, I forgave.

When my son was killed in January 1983, sorrow, "like a mighty wave, swept all my pride away," and I realized that as never before, I was able to forgive someone who had hurt me deeply. It made me see how, in one more way, the death of someone we love can change us, not from what we were, so much as toward what we essentially are—loving, forgiving people.

Which leads to the next point: what are we to say when someone dies too soon, of an accident, of cancer, of AIDS? One thing we must never say is that it is the will of God. No one knows that for sure, so let no one pretend he or she does. Why would it be the will of God that a particular person die young, while the rest of us live on? What we *can* say are St. Paul's words, "Love never ends"; because as St. Paul also says, "I am persuaded that neither death nor life . . . can separate us from the love of God" (Rom. 8:38). In other words, the abyss of love is deeper than the abyss of death. That means our own loves—pale reflections of God's love—are right to reject death. And we can say more: The seers and saints, those most attentive to God's presence in this word, have always claimed that the best lies ahead. Bach entitled one of his greatest arias, "Komm, süsser Tod" (Come Sweet Death) and an American slave saw "a band of angels coming for to carry me home."

Of course, life after death can no more be proved than disproved. "For nothing worth proving can be proven, nor yet disproven" as Tennyson said. As a child in a womb cannot conceive of life with air and light—the very stuff of our existence—so it is hard for us to conceive of any other life without the sustaining forces to which we are accustomed. But consider this: If we are essentially spirit, not flesh, if what is substantial is intangible, if we are spirits that have bodies and not the other way around; then it makes sense that just as musicians can abandon their instruments to find others elsewhere, so at death our spirits can leave our bodies and find other forms in which to make new music.

And one more thought: Love is its own reward. For its

inspiration, love does not depend on the pay it receives, which is why, out of hand, we have to reject all notions of heaven as pie in the sky by and by—deferred gratification. (I hate the way some evangelists try to overcome my selfishness by appealing to my selfish motives!) But the fact of the matter is, love does have a reward. Just as the proper benefits of education are the opportunites of continuing education, so the rewards of loving are to become yet more vulnerable, more tender, more caring. It is also a fact that human life aspires beyond its grasp. As God led Moses to the mountaintop, so life leads us to a place where we can view a land that is promised but never reached. To me, it is hard to believe that a loving God would create loving creatures who aspire to be yet more loving, and then finish them off before their aspirations are complete. There must be something more.

But again, we don't know the circumstances. We know only who, not what, is beyond the grave. This side of the grave, we are like the Swiss child asked by a traveler, "Where is Kandesteg?" The child answered, "I cannot tell you where Kandesteg is, but there is the road." We are on the road to heaven if today we walk with God. Eternal life is not a possession conferred at death, it is a present endowment. We live it now, and continue it through death.

Death is not the enemy. If death enhances both our individual and common life, and if death is no threat to our relationship with God, then death is more friend than foe. The good news is, "Whether we live or whether we die, we are the Lord's" (Rom. 14:8).

# 23. A Present-Day Reformation

Reading:    Matthew 25:31–46

That the churches could better the lot of humanity, even save the world, goes without saying. The only question is whether Christians in sufficient number will find the imagination and dedication, in the coming decades, to effect a reformation comparable in scope and influence to the sixteenth-century one we celebrate yearly. Today I'd like to sketch the outline of such a reformation, and in so doing acknowledge my indebtedness to, among others, Harvey Cox and Robert McAfee Brown.

The reform in our day should start with what I have often complained of as the "privatization" of Christianity, which severs *homo religiosus* from *homo politicus* and produces, among its unfortunate offspring, a spiritual schizophrenia in the individual, a trivializing of the Christian faith, and the abandonment of the public domain to the toughest powermongers around.

It is interesting to trace our progress to this sorry state of affairs. Over the recent centuries there have been many political revolutions, most of them middle class, which in the name of liberty succeeded in stripping religious institutions of the worldly powers they long exercised. At the same time that church and state were being separated, universities, long wed to the churches, began divorce proceedings. Thus was set in motion a whole process of secularization, which gradually took over everything in the public domain: government, universities, schools, hospitals, businesses—the works. And in many ways this was a good thing, for by and large the churches were too worldly and too reactionary, too tied to an old and passing order.

But today, with the benefit of hindsight, we can see that this process of secularization had as much to do with power as with the freedom in whose name it was undertaken. For now nation-states are free to demand complete loyalty to themselves without regard to anyone, even to God. Financiers are free to make money without the moral restraints imposed by religion. Universities are free to exalt the right of the individual to think and do almost anything over any obligation to do good. And the churches, with no real function for society as a whole, have been relegated to the role of comforting people in this world and preparing them for the next. Oh, they can tell their members to be kind and honest within established structures, but they are no more expected to change these structures than they were expected, during the Middle Ages, to alter the feudal relationships between the nobility and their serfs.

So the churches that once helped to keep royalty in power by being themselves too worldly, are today keeping the middle class in power by being too other-worldly.

Is this good for the middle class? I think not. I think that by supporting—if only by not protesting—the political and economic goals of their middle-class members, the churches are killing them spiritually. In the United States, *The Reader's Digest* offers a case in point. This is a publication that has probably warmed the cockles of more middle-class hearts than any other publication in America, a magazine that is generally viewed as comfy, earnest, optimistic, a patriotic defender of the national faith. Yet its November 1983 issue featured the following five articles: "How to stay slim forever," "Five ways to stop feeling tired," "How to get your way," "How safe are the new contraceptives?" and "What it takes to be successful." It would appear that the editors have concluded that their millions of readers are—consecutively—fat, lazy, frustrated, lascivious, and unsuccessful. The thought that the editors might be right, that we are indeed a nation of autoerotic stumble-bums, is enough to chill the heart.

But even more damaging than the spiritual slaughter of their middle-class members is the churches' neglect of the vast majority of the human race who are anything but middle class—who are, in fact, wretchedly poor. And so the reformation I envision calls for the churches, which once supported royalty, and then supported the bourgeoisie, to take up today the cause of the poor—and for the sake of the rich as well as the poor. I think that the challenge for the churches today is to shake off reliance on privilege, and to heed the invitation offered in 1968 by the Roman Catholic bishops of Latin America: "We invite all, without distinction of class, to accept and take up the cause of the poor, as if they were accepting and taking up their own cause, the very cause of Jesus Christ." I think that the challenge for Christians today is to learn as did Dietrich Bonhoeffer in Nazi prisons, "to see the great events of world history from below, from the perspective of the outcasts, the suspects, the maltreated, the powerless, the oppressed, the reviled—in short, from the perspective of those who suffer" (from *Letters and Papers from Prison*).

Believing that the world is going to be changed from the bottom up and from the edges in, I think we have to put an end not only to "trickle-down" economics but to "trickle-down" theology, which has become largely irrelevant. We need a theology steeped in justice, one which reminds the nations that "Inasmuch as ye have done it unto one of the least of these my brethren, ye have done it unto me" (Matt. 25:40)—for the parable is addressed to the nations ("and before him shall be gathered all nations" Matt. 25:32). We need a theology that knits together *homo religiosus* and *homo politicus*, so that Christians can once again see how theological and biblical insights relate to public life as well as to private life. We need a theology that sees sin not only in personal but also in institutional form, for the principal actors in today's world are nations, business enterprises, political and economic groups of one kind and another. We need a theology that reminds the universities, in the old Calvinist phrase, that "truth is in order to goodness," that the acquisition of knowledge is second to its use. We need a theology that has good things to say for anger, because if you lower your quotient of anger against oppression you lower your quotient of love for the oppressed. We need a theology that sees Jesus not only as our personal Savior and founder of the Church, but also as saving grace for the whole world. And we need to see the Church not only as an institution, but as a community of God's people, a community that envisions salvation as an Exodus for all humanity in which all forms of injustice will be left behind.

We need, in short, a theology of compassion. For a world that is going to be changed from the bottom up and the edges in, we need a theology that starts at the bottom of everyone's heart and works its way up to the top of everyone's head.

There is, of course, a danger in all this—the danger of politicizing the faith, of churches overly committing themselves to dubious or mistaken political causes. It is one thing to say, "Let justice roll down like mighty waters" (Amos 5:24), and quite another to work out the irrigation system. Clearly, there is more certainty in the recognition of wrongs, than there is in the prescriptions for the cure of those wrongs. For example, it is clear that the arms race has to end or the human race probably will. But if Christ is dead-set against the arms race— as I am sure Christ is—there is no Christ-given program for how worldwide disarmament should proceed. It is also clear that American fear of Marxism has blinded most Americans to the failures of capitalism in Central America. In El Salvador, Guatemala, Honduras, present economic structures generously benefit a minority while leaving unattended the most basic needs of the impoverished majority. In these countries the pyramid of society has to be turned upside down—not just a new top put on. But that is not to say that the Cubans and the Sandinistas, who have seriously tried to turn pyramids upside down, have come up with all the right programmatic answers.

Gustavo Gutierrez, the Peruvian theologian, says in *A Theology of Liberation* that the church has a "prophetic function of denouncing every injustice," of living in "authentic solidarity with the poor," and making "a real protest against the poverty of our time." Yet Gutierrez adds, "My personal option for the socialist way is not a conclusion drawn from evangelical premises. It comes from my socio-political analysis."

There are two things about that statement that strike me. In the first place Gutierrez implies what is true, that the Bible rarely prescribes the specific political and economic patterns required by God's love. The few times the Bible does get specific—as in the Deuteronomic and Levitical laws, or in St. Paul's treatment of how women are supposed to behave—it is probably least useful for our present, very different historical situation. Contrary to Fundamentalists, I believe God leads with a light rein, giving us our head. To be sure Jesus gives concrete examples of wrong-doing and right-doing, as in the story of the Good Samaritan; but he speaks in parables precisely because stories have a way of shifting responsibility from the narrator to the hearer. In short, Jesus gives us, if you will, our marching orders—"to set at liberty those who are oppressed"—but he leaves it to us to figure out the route of march. And that leads me to the second thing I like in Gutierrez's statement: He has figured out a march route, he has a "socio-political analysis." We may not embrace his, at least not 100 percent, but it may well be that God wants us to struggle for one of our own, lest our faith become divorced from action.

Why do I say that? Because our present system, however we label it, simply is not working, and largely because we Christians worship God in our "spiritual" life and mammon in our economic life. The system is not working when the answer to New York's homeless is not a home, but a shelter or a motel in New Jersey. The system is not working when hunger is on the rise, yes, in the richest nation of the world. The system is not working when 70 to 80 percent of all released prisoners return to prison, and generally for worse crimes. The system is certainly not working abroad when no end to the arms race is in sight; and when throughout Central and Latin America, and South Africa as well, the United States has seemingly nothing to offer the millions who are tired of being unemployed, underfed, ill without money to buy medicines—nothing, that is, except the prospect of more dead, mutilated bodies in their streets. American Christians shudder at the prospect of Marxist influences in the churches. They should watch equally devout Christians from third world countries shudder at words like capitalism, neocolonialism, and transnational corporations. They may not be right, these third world Christians, in all their conclusions, but they are right to have what Gutierrez calls "my socio-political analysis." Without such an analysis, how are we going to translate the story of the Good Samaritan into terms that make sense in New York and Chicago? Without such an analysis, how are we going to set at liberty those who are oppressed at home and abroad?

Let us not be confused about what is meant by the separation of church and state. The doctrine is a sound one, but the separation it talks about is an organizational one. The separation of church and state is not designed to separate Christians from their politics.

Let me conclude with an image of the Church that often comes to mind during Holy Communion. After breaking the bread, Jesus said, "Take, eat, this is my body which is broken for you." But the bread is not only a symbol of Jesus; it is also symbolic of the Church, which calls itself "the body of Christ." In other words, as members of Christ's church, Christians are brought together in one loaf to be broken to feed the world.

As I said at the beginning: That the churches could better the lot of humanity, even save the world, goes without saying. The only question is whether we will.

# Index

# Date Due